THE *Art* OF
WOMANHOOD

Teaching Your Man How To Love
You The Way You Want To Be
Loved Without Him Knowing He's
Being Taught!

BOOK ONE

Frank E. Legette III

Publishing Services provided by Paper Raven Books LLC

Printed in the United States of America

First Printing, 2023

Paperback ISBN: 979-8-9879867-2-1
Hardback ISBN: 979-8-9879867-1-4
Ebook ISBN: 979-8-9879867-0-7

Copyright # 1-909817671

Email: info@theartofwomanhood.org

DEDICATION

This book has been 18 years in the making. I dedicate it to my daughter Kesha, who first suggested that I put on paper the things I was teaching her, my wife Angela, my mother Ora, my friend Ebelin, and all the women who motivated, inspired, and urged me to write and finish this book and share my knowledge with women everywhere. I thank you for being consistent and persistent.

TABLE OF CONTENTS

INTRODUCTION

From the outset, I want you to know that I'm convinced that women are the most incredible people on the planet. In fact, it's not even close.

Furthermore, I want you to consider that the characteristics of a typical woman are closer to the characteristics of God than the typical man. Examine the fruit of the Spirit, which are nine characteristics of the Holy Spirit—who is a member of the Godhead. In other words, He's God. Take a careful look at these nine fruit: love, joy, peace, patience, kindness, goodness, faithfulness, gentleness, and self-control.

Now, let's take a look at women. They are loving, joyful, peaceful, patient, kind, good, faithful, and gentle. The last is showing self-control. Do women always exhibit self-control? No. But then again, if men did the right thing and treated them the way they deserve, they wouldn't spiral out of control. When women lose it, it's usually because men have pushed their buttons so much that they feel backed into a corner, and thus they come out fighting.

Now, I'm not trying to make all women out to be saints. However, the average woman is far superior in character to the average man because a woman more closely resembles the character of God. Is it any wonder that the symbol for the church in scripture is a woman and not a man? Isn't that interesting?

Why would God choose a woman to be the face of His church? It's simple: Christ wanted His church to reflect the same characteristics to mankind that women display daily. The Master knew that if the church exhibited womanly characteristics, His church, though small at its inception, would ultimately explode and circle the globe with its power and influence.

You are the apple of God's eye. Unfortunately, you consistently are the last one to realize it. When you do, you will realize how incredible you are, and your self-confidence will soar into the stratosphere.

When that happens, how you view yourself and what you accept and tolerate from men will change. When you recognize your value and worth, you will begin the process of transitioning into the woman God has always destined you to be.

Please know that I have dedicated my life to helping you to accomplish God's will for your life. Nothing, and I mean nothing, would make me happier. Let's do it!

CHAPTER 1

THE PHONE CALL THAT CHANGED MY LIFE

The Spark of an Idea

How did I come to write a book for women and have a ministry that is exclusively for women? Here is how this journey began, quite ironically, I might add.

I picked up the phone one previously uneventful day and dialed one of my daughters. Little did I know at the time, but it was a call that would change my life forever.

I heard the dial tone; then the phone rang three, four, five times. My daughter finally answered, but what I heard stopped me dead in my tracks. She was crying. Correction: she was bawling. She could barely speak. She struggled to say hello. I stopped in the middle of my kitchen. Without her ever saying a word, I knew the source of her intense, searing pain.

You see, no one loves like a woman—no one! A woman loves the only way she knows how, which is with every fiber of her being. And when a woman loves a man, she gives him her very best. So when a woman takes off her clothes, lies down, and takes in her man, she is saying, "I'm giving you the best I have." For a woman, it is the ultimate statement.

But when that man takes her love, tosses it on the ground, and tramples on it, for her there is no greater disrespect. There is no greater pain.

Without her saying another word, I knew what the problem was. I stood there, in the middle of the floor, thinking, "This can't be happening to my daughter."

As a result of pastoring for, at that particular point, 20 years, I've had many occasions where a woman approaches me at church and says, "Pastor, I need to talk to you."

"Sure," I respond, and off we head to my office for some privacy.

In the office, I direct her to a chair nearest the door while I pull up another chair to face her directly. No sooner than I turn and am seated, the tears will begin to trickle down her face. Quite often, the floodgates open before she's even said a word. As soon as the tears begin to fall, I already know her painful saga. In fact, I can tell her her own story.

Sadly, it always goes something like this: she met a guy. He wined her and dined her. Desperate to be loved, she compromised her Biblical principles. She moved him in, knowing her actions were in violation of everything she stood for. She treated him like a king. He wanted for nothing. She supplied him with all the sex he could endure, sumptuous meals, new clothes, and money in his pocket.

And quite often, he stayed in her house while she went to work. In fact, before long, he was driving her car while she caught the bus or rides from her friends.

And then it happened. Somehow, she discovered his dirty little secret. Not only was he cheating on her, but he was bringing other women to her house and having sex with them in her bed. She was devastated. I had heard it countless times.

And now here I was, standing with the phone to my ear, knowing that my daughter was so knee-deep in mess that it was breaking my heart. I had no idea how or why she was there.

But this much was obvious: she had chased him, wined him, dined him, and pampered him. She waited on him hand and foot, but he did not cherish the gift.

She, too, was devastated. Although she was feeling the lion's share of that pain, I, her father, was not painless. I hurt because I had failed in protecting the daughter, whom I loved dearly, from a wolf in sheep's clothing. I had failed in warning her not to violate God's word because it would come back to haunt her. I didn't fulfill my duties and responsibilities as a father in safeguarding my child. I shared her pain because I shared her guilt.

After standing there silently, for what seemed like hours but what in reality had only been seconds, wishing I could instantly wipe away her tears and repair her broken heart, I said to her, "When you get sick and tired of being sick and tired, call me. I'll fix this for you."

Six months passed. Then one day, my phone rang. It was my daughter.

She said, "Pop Pop, I'm ready."

I said, "Okay, hold out your hand—palm up."

"What?" she said.

I repeated it. "Hold out your hand so you see the white part of your hand."

I could feel the frown on her face.

"Is your hand out?" I asked.

"Yes," she replied.

I said, "If you do what I tell you to do, when I tell you to do it, and how I tell you to do it, you'll have that brother right there in the palm of your hand in a minute."

"Get out of here," she said.

I declared confidently, "If you do what I tell you to do, then he's going to respond exactly the way I tell you. And when you call me to tell me that it went down exactly the way I described it I'm going to try not to say—I really can't guarantee it—but I'll try not to say, 'I told you so.' So, are you ready?"

"Yes," she said.

"Okay, here's what I want you to do," I said.

I explained to her how to use the "Nutcracker Technique," which I now teach to women in my empowerment classes. This technique is one that every woman needs to have in their arsenal when their man declares that "it's over" or that he "wants a divorce" because he's "found someone else."

I declared emphatically that if anything could restore my daughter's broken relationship, this one technique could.

Most importantly, I taught my daughter the psychology associated with the technique. She hung up the phone and called the brother and implemented the technique perfectly. I must confess that she is arguably the best student I have ever had.

In less than an hour, she called me and declared excitedly, "Pop Pop, it works."

I tried—no, for real, seriously, I tried. I tried not to say, "I told you so," but I failed, and I just blurted out, "I tried to tell you!"

She informed me that she called the brother and did the technique flawlessly, just like I taught her.

Within 20 minutes, he was knocking at her door and saying, "What do you mean it's over? It's not over."

She informed him, in no uncertain terms, that it was.

Instantly, her life had been altered. Instantly, she had her dignity and self-esteem, which had suffered for months, restored because she was in a relationship that was upside down. She was in violation of God's clearly defined rules.

Because of one technique, she went from being powerless to powerful. She went from being the pursuer to being the pursued. She went from being the bee to being an awesome flower, which is exactly what God determined that women should be in their relationships with men.

She was elated. She felt good. She felt liberated. Instantly, the roles had been reversed, and she was now right side up in her relationship—exactly where God wanted her to be. Being able to walk away from a relationship that she now realized was never in her best interest in the first place was terribly empowering.

She then made the statement that changed my life forever.

She said, "Pop Pop, you need to write a book because women don't know this stuff."

I was blown away. No one had ever said that to me. In lieu of writing the book, I began to work with her and share my concepts and techniques that I had been using for the past two-and-a-half decades.

In addition to that, I immediately went to my Women's Ministry Director, Masego Kebaetse, and informed her that I had some information that might be beneficial to the women of our church. I shared with her my experience with my daughter, and she was intrigued. She called the women together, and I did my first presentation. They were amazed—married and single, younger and older alike. It was my first real public test, and I knew that I was on to something.

As a result, I've dedicated my life to empowering and liberating women and teaching these life-changing techniques. Very few things in life give me more pleasure than to have a woman call me and scream in my ear, "It works!"

A Community of Women

My wife, Angela, and I were sitting in our living room in Winter Park, Florida when the doorbell rang one Sunday morning. It was Esther Pond. She had come to visit Sherma, a young lady who was staying with us on a temporary basis. In the midst of the conversation, Sherma suggested that Esther inquire about the women's ministry that I conduct.

Esther turned and said, "Talk to me."

For the next few minutes, I shared several concepts. Her eyes widened with anticipation.

When I finished, she said, "Pastor Legette, the women of Patmos need your help. Will you work with us?"

"I'd be delighted to," I answered.

"How many women do you need for us to get started?" she asked. I informed her that 10 would be a good number.

That next Sabbath afternoon, right after church, 10 women walked through my front door. On the spot, the "Flower Training Academy" (which would evolve into The Women's Empowerment HQ) was launched.

I worked with them for eight weeks. About half of them were married or had been, while the other half were single.

At the conclusion of the eighth session, as I was about to leave Florida and return to my pastoral duties in Pennsylvania, the ladies shared their testimonies with my wife and me.

As a result of sharing what they deemed to be life-changing information, they also wanted me to teach their daughters, relatives, and friends—many of whom were located all over the country.

I began to conduct weekly webinars. At the end of each webinar, I'd conduct a Q & A session. Consequently, I've arrived at this sad but true conclusion: for some reason that I can only speculate about, decades ago, mothers stopped passing down the requisite knowledge their daughters needed as they entered their twenties and began dating.

Far too many women in their late teens, early twenties, and even in their thirties and forties, have no idea how to be in a relationship with a man and get what they want and need to be happy in that relationship. Worse yet, many, if not most of them, are completely incapable of either recognizing a brother's game or how to adroitly counteract his game with a skillset of their own.

Millions of maturing young women enter the dating game every year truly unprepared for that eventuality. That is both sad but true. Instantly, they are at a distinct disadvantage.

To what would I liken a young woman who's just entering the dating world? I'd liken her to a helpless, harmless, inexperienced wildebeest calf in the heart of the jungle who's been separated from its mother and the herd.

As the skillful, vastly experienced, and starving lions move in for the kill, literally, the calf is alone and confused. It doesn't know what to do or how to fend for itself. It calls for its mother—no answer. It hasn't been taught how to fend off hungry predators. And now it's too late, for within seconds, the pack has ripped this once-cute little animal into pieces as they gorge themselves on its carcass and fight over its remains.

Our young women are needlessly facing similar experiences every day because they are facing vastly more experienced men while they themselves are at the opposite end of the experience spectrum.

While there are several contributing factors, there is one factor that far outweighs all the others: very few older women are teaching young women, especially in their formative years, how to deal with men.

For the most part, the knowledge that used to be imparted to young women has long since been absent from the picture. For that reason, young women of all races, colors, creeds, and religions, end up in such deplorable situations.

And quite often, they have no idea how they got there.

Invariably, these women fail to understand that guys detect inexperience in women like dogs detect fear in humans! When the average guy sees an innocent, inexperienced, untrained, young lady who's ill-equipped to adequately handle or recognize his "game," he salivates because he knows that it will be like taking candy from a baby. What's even sadder is that the younger and more inexperienced she is, the more ecstatic he becomes.

Let me compound the situation further. Women who are never properly taught how to be in a relationship with a man more often than not raise daughters quite ill-prepared to deal with that which is coming their way.

But my question is why? It's simple: you can't teach what you've never learned.

As I address women from across the country, I'm often shocked and surprised to encounter women of all ages, in society at large as well as in the church, that have never been taught how to use their God-given gifts to get what they need from the men in their lives. These women run the gamut from the youngest to the oldest amongst us, from the least to the most professional, and all in between.

While guys are honing their skills in the street, females, on the other hand, generally, are sheltered and protected by parents at home doing the things they've been trained to do: cooking, cleaning, and looking after younger siblings.

So when the street-smart brother, who has been sexually active for years—as evidenced by the one or two children that he's previously fathered—meets you or your relationally inexperienced daughter, I'll give you one guess as to who wins and who loses in that scenario.

So, what's the solution?

Here it is: someone must teach young women how to fend for themselves. Someone who truly understands how a man thinks and who knows the game he will run needs to emerge and provide women with the knowledge and information that will not just educate them, but liberate and empower them to be all that God would have them to be.

Within the context of these pages I will, to the best of my ability, do just that. I will educate, enlighten, inform, and implore, but more importantly, my goal is to equip women with the tools and the techniques that they must have to experience the kind of happiness that they desire in their relationship with men.

Permit me to make this personal. For the next several days, weeks, months, or however long it takes you to read this book from cover to cover, I'll show you how to master YOUR God-given gifts, which are designed to even the playing field in your relationship.

If you apply yourself and take the information to heart, I will teach you how to master the all-important but forgotten art of womanhood.

I will not, although I could, spend time exposing the brothers' games. That would be a frivolous endeavor. Here's why: men are no match for women who have mastered the art of womanhood.

I'll teach you how to master the gifts that God has given you to ensure your relational happiness. Moreover, I will also teach you how to teach your man to love you the way you want to be loved—without him even knowing it!

When you can do that, you have arrived at MASTER status, and that's exactly what this book is designed to help you become.

And guess what, ladies? There's nothing men can do to stop it—even if they read this book themselves!

Some of you are thinking, "How can a man teach a woman how to master the art of womanhood? Only a woman can teach another woman how to do that."

Let me be honest with you. Prior to the experience I had with my own daughter that launched this ministry, I would have agreed with you. However, when God taps you on the shoulder and says, "Do this for me," you do it, no matter if it makes sense or not.

Therefore, from the word of God and from personal experiences—some good, some bad—I'm going to share with you God's blueprint for womanhood.

My goal is to help you become the kind of woman that God has destined you to be. And in the end, when you've completed this book or attended any of **The Women's Empowerment HQ presentations**, you will be amazed at the information you have received, the wisdom of how to use it, the power you have amassed, and the confidence you possess. Are you ready for the journey? Then, let's go!

Action Plan
FOR CHAPTER 1

For each chapter, I want you to develop an action plan to implement the lessons I reviewed. This is a time to reflect, assess your personal romantic relationships, and start to take steps to empower yourself along this journey.

1. Find a family member or friend who will always tell you the truth, no matter how badly it hurts. Consult that person when you meet a new man. Keep quiet and listen to them. If they love you, they will tell you the truth. A part of your inner circle should always be a female. Find one who is trustworthy and protects your privacy. She will have an intuition that males do not possess. She will sense and detect things that could elude you. Listen to them.

2. For those ladies who are still single, consult my website (theartofwomanhood.org) and download the document, "5 Things A Woman Should Never Do On A First Date."

3. Never permit yourself to become so desperate to have a man that you accept anything from him just to have a man on your arm. Desperate women get used and

abused, and it's not cute. Talk to the Lord. He knows what you want and need. Pray. Fast. Be patient and wait on Him. You can trust Him.

4. Need to talk? Send me an email at thewomensempowermenthq@gmail.com, and I will schedule a 30-minute consultation with you.

CHAPTER 2

WARNING! YOUR MARRIAGE/ RELATIONSHIP MAY BE HAZARDOUS TO YOUR HEALTH!

Embrace the Reality

Your mission, should you choose to accept, it is to get your man to love you the way you want to be loved. Period. End of discussion! And, before you ask the question, I'm going to answer by declaring emphatically that your life and your longevity on this planet may literally depend on it.

You cannot afford to fail in this endeavor. If you don't understand anything else from this book, I need you to get this: your man—your husband or boyfriend—must learn to love you on your terms, not his!

I'll be very frank with you; you're going to have to help him embrace this concept. Make no mistake about it, for most men this concept is a radical and foreign departure from how they've loved in the past and how they intend to love you in the present and the future.

The truth of the matter is many of you are in unhappy relationships. For those of you who find yourself in this unfortunate situation, it's not always because your companion is not a good man. It's probably because he doesn't know how to love you the way you want to be loved, and he may not know any other way to love you.

Many of you have been talking, begging, or pleading with your man to treat you differently. He may think that you're being overly sensitive. He may declare that he's always treated his women this way. Or, worse yet, he may state that if he knew you were the type of wife who was never satisfied with the way he loves or treats you, then he would have made someone else his wife.

I know. I used to be one of those men who made ignorant statements like that. The typical man wants to think that he knows how to love his woman. When you tell a man that the way that he loves you is unacceptable, he won't take that well. It's painful for a man to hear that he doesn't know how to love you—that what he's offering is not good enough! No man wants to hear that. Most men will be angered at that notion, will not want to have that conversation, and might shut down on you.

He, in fact, might accuse you, as I did my wife, of being the kind of woman who can't be satisfied, or is too needy, or, worse yet, is too picky. He may retort that there is nothing wrong with the way he loves. He may reply in anger that it was good enough for all the other women he's been with, so how in the world could it not be good enough for you? You might hear that if he became a free man, those women would be on him like a bum on a baloney sandwich.

Listen to me and listen carefully—you and you alone are the one and only expert on Planet Earth when it comes to knowing how you want to be loved. And if you say it's not acceptable, then it's not acceptable.

When you declare that you don't feel loved, for many of you, it's probably not that he doesn't love you at all. It could be that he's not loving you the way YOU want to be loved. You have the last word as to whether he hits a home run or strikes out in the love department.

My friend and mentor Vernon Dawson, co-founder of The Voice In The Wilderness Mission in Savoy, Massachusetts, asked his wife, Sheree, if she was happy one day. She said "no." After she thought about it, she informed him that she knew he loved her, but she didn't "feel" loved. He asked the question because he was self-assured that he was doing and had done all the things he was supposed to do as a man to make his wife happy. He only asked because he was confident the answer was going to be positive. You see, he was loving her the way he thought he should love her. Fortunately for him, he asked.

When he discovered that she was not happy, he asked her what would make her happy. She informed him, and to his credit, he changed. He began the process of loving her the way she wanted to be loved. When men successfully achieve that goal, their wives are extremely happy because they are being loved on their terms.

If every man replicated Vernon's actions and loved you on your terms and not his—they'd get it right every time without fail.

If all men embraced this challenge, there would be far fewer unhappy marriages and relationships. There would be less divorce and fewer broken homes. More children would grow up with both parents and thus receive the love, care, and instruction from those parents under the same roof, which is what God destined them to receive.

As a result, many of our children would reach adulthood having received from both parents what they need to be mature, fully developed adults, ready to take on a life partner of their own. Wow, all of that would be achievable. If we could only love that way, we would change the world! But, unfortunately, we are not there yet, and we've got a long way to go to get there. This book is an attempt to bridge that gap.

Your Health Is at Risk

Ladies, when you inform him that he's not loving you in a way that pleases and satisfies you, and he's angered by that, shuts down, and refuses to talk about it, you cannot—you must not—acquiesce and declare, "Well, I guess this is what I'm going to have to live with."

No! You cannot embrace that mindset because you will suffer in more ways than one. The tragic reality is that if you do not acquire a different skillset that enables you to approach this delicate subject skillfully, then you may never receive the kind of love that you deserve. As a result, true love and ultimate fulfillment will be terribly elusive to you. The closest that many of you will come to being loved on your terms is, sadly enough, in your dreams.

And once you wake and the dream is over, the nightmare begins. In fact, it is a most disturbing reality that some women will die and go into the grave dreaming of the love they deserve without ever achieving it in their entire lifetime.

The Bible is clear when it states, "A merry heart doeth good like a medicine: but a broken spirit drieth the bones." (Prov. 17:22).

Again, I recall my friends Vernon and Sheree, of The Voice In The Wilderness Mission. When referring to the negative aspect of this passage, they refer to it as "a broken heart and a broken spirit."

It was at their mission—a health sanitarium where incredible healing takes place in 10 days, all without drugs—that I heard the Dawsons say this regarding their clients who had gone through their program.

At the end of their stay, their clients' vitals were perfect, their symptoms had disappeared, their pains had vanished, and the healing process was well underway after a mere 10 days. But shortly after some of the clients returned home, those same symptoms and problems were back with a vengeance.

Why? It was because many of them, and this is especially true of the women, returned home to toxic marriages and relationships. Tragically, as I enquired about the women that I'd met there, I learned that not long after they returned home, their health again deteriorated rapidly. My wife and I even befriended some of them. We kept in contact for a while. But a number of these women lost the fight and eventually died.

They were beautiful women. They were extraordinary women. They were wives, mothers, grandmothers, sisters, and daughters. They were all that and then some. They desperately wanted to live. But they were so unhappy, so miserable, so unloved that a door was cracked open, and in walked life-threatening illnesses and diseases—most notably cancer.

Ladies, do you know what happens when you are stressed, depressed, angry, cheated on, disrespected, publicly embarrassed, and put on Front Street?

There are two main hormones the body secretes when it perceives a threat, whether mental or physical, acute or chronic.

Acute threats are temporary, short-term threats, like when someone jumps out of the darkness and frightens you. Your body immediately secretes adrenaline and cortisol—the flight-or-fight hormones—to give you the energy and strength to get out of harm's way.

Conversely, chronic threats are long-lasting threats that continue for days, weeks, months, even years. However, neither adrenaline nor cortisol were designed by God to be secreted long-term. Why not? The effects can be deadly—especially to women.

Herein lies the problem. When women, in particular, are in a toxic, stressful, relationship, these hormones, like a leaky faucet, are continuously being secreted.

Dr. Don Colbert, in his book *Deadly Emotions*, states: "The perpetual release of the stress hormones adrenaline and cortisol can sear the body in a way that is similar to acid searing metal." [1] In other words, continuous stress to the body is like drinking acid!

---

1 Dr. Don Colbert, *Deadly Emotions*, Thomas Nelson Publishers: Nashville, p. 17

In another excellent book, *When The Body Says No*, Dr. Gabor Maté makes the cogent argument that there is a direct correlation between stress and disease which often leads to cancer and other diseases.

He writes: "But the same stress responses triggered chronically and without resolution produce harm and even permanent damage. Chronically high cortisol levels destroy tissue. Chronically elevated adrenaline levels raise the blood pressure and damage the heart." [2]

Not only does Dr. Maté reveal a correlation between stress and cancer, repressed anger, heart disease, high blood pressure, and osteoporosis, he also points out there is a stress and MS connection when he states that "About 60% of those affected are women." [3]

Stress is a killer! Consequently, when women are emotionally, verbally, and physically abused, or are brokenhearted and constantly bickering, their bodies secrete harmful levels of adrenaline and cortisol that severely impairs their health and puts their lives in jeopardy.

Dr. Maté also notes that "Research has suggested for decades that women are more prone to develop breast cancer if their childhoods were characterized by emotional disconnection from their parents or other disturbances in their [upbringing]." [4]

It's tragic how many men fail to understand that when their girlfriends and wives are brokenhearted, unhappy, and mistreated, they often send them to an early grave.

---

2 Dr. Gabor Maté, *When The Body Says No*, John Wiley & Sons Inc.: Hoboken, New Jersey, p. 33

3 Dr. Gabor Maté, *When The Body Says No*, p. 62

4 Dr. Gabor Maté, *When The Body Says No*, p. 16

All they wanted was to be loved. Not just any love would suffice, however. They merely wanted to be loved the way they needed to be loved. They wanted the kind of love that they had consistently given for years and, in many cases, decades. Was that too much to ask from their men? How could it be if these men claimed to love them? How could that be an imposition after all the sacrifices these women made on their behalf? How could it be too much to ask when many of these women slaved and worked in obscurity or worked their fingers to the bone so that their men could get their degrees or build their businesses while the women single-handedly took care of the home and the children?

When women are not loved, it can leave them physically and emotionally vulnerable and particularly susceptible to life-threatening disease. After 60-plus years of being on this planet and 40-plus years of pastoring, I'm truly sick and tired of watching—and burying—beautiful women as they die of a broken heart.

Women must be loved. And when they aren't, the consequences can be both devastating and deadly. A real-world example should suffice.

For the sake of privacy, let's call her Tara. She was young, beautiful, vibrant, full of life, talented, and in love. She was a loving wife. She had everything to live for, except she didn't. She died in the prime of her life. It was tragic. It was painful to watch. It was ugly.

She insisted on receiving from her husband the type of love she had always given him. She could not get past the affair he had with another woman. She was determined to be loved the way she wanted to be loved—to be loved the way she had loved him. She was relentless in her quest for happiness. She insisted on being the one and only recipient of his affections. Despite all her complaints, all her tears and pleas, in spite of her tantrums and threats, she continued to go unloved. If she had written a screenplay of her life, the title of her biopic would have been "An Unrequited Love."

The affair was all-consuming to her. It was a veritable nightmarish albatross around her neck. She couldn't shake it. She couldn't get past it. If you were a part of her inner circle, she talked about it openly, freely, often. The reminders were everywhere, reminding her not of his failures, but hers. It was a slap in her face, not his. It said, in so many words, that she was not good enough, sexy enough, pretty enough.

The very notion of her man making love to and giving another woman that which she knew belonged exclusively to her was unconscionable to her. It was like a huge hunting knife that was thrust through her heart and, to add insult to injury, was left in place, forcing her to attempt to somehow manage that immense, searing, unbearable pain while still being required to take care of his needs as if everything were okay when everything was certainly not.

She stewed in it day by day, week by week, month by month. She created a mental picture—a movie if you will—of the affair. And when the movie ended, she replayed it as if it would end differently this time around, or, better yet, as if this time she was the paramour. Sadly, it never did. Tragically, she never was. She was stuck.

The very thought of sharing her man was literally killing her. Rather than begging, pleading, and fussing, if she had negotiated from a position of strength and left, if only temporarily, perhaps her story would have had a better outcome. Perhaps she'd be alive today.

Even when the affair ended, it remained a topic of conversation constantly—morning, noon, and night. No one can dwell in an emotional cesspool without suffering consequences.

Then she received the dreaded news—cancer! Because of the emotional trauma that was bombarding her body, no one should have been surprised—no one. Ladies, you can't exist on an emotional battlefield for an extended period of time without consequences. The stress alone is devastating to the human body.

Cancer was running roughshod through her body like a bull in a china shop, and yet she could not let go, move on, and focus on her health and wellbeing. She wanted to be loved by the man she had given herself to. She wanted to be the one and only apple of his eye. She wanted to know that she and she alone was the recipient of his love and affections. She refused not to be loved by him, even though it was obvious it was not to be.

Why didn't she just leave? Why couldn't she put herself, her life, and her heath first? It's easy to judge when you haven't been in that situation. I know; I was there. In my first marriage, while fighting for the relationship, I became a doormat. Who, me? Yes, me.

Why? How? It really is simple. Notwithstanding that choosing a life's partner is one of the most important decisions you'll ever make, no one, and I mean no one, is taught what to do when your marital ship is sinking. So, practically, everything I did drove her further into the arms of the other guy.

Finally, when you're fighting for your family, style points don't matter. We, the unloved, are willing to make any sacrifice to keep our families intact—even when we look weak in the process.

The cancer attacked Tara like a ravenous wolf, like a raging flood, like a starving pit bull pouncing on a plate of food. It was relentless. It was aggressive. It was, to say the least, deadly.

She died wanting one thing: to be loved the way she wanted to be loved. She died without ever experiencing it. How tragic.

Over the last 40 years of ministry, I've been privileged to meet some awesome women. And, over that period of time, I've watched in horror as some of them have developed one life-threatening illness after another. For these particular women, their stories are eerily similar.

They are as follows:

1. They suffered in silence. Many have been unhappy for years, even decades. Some have never known happiness in their marriage/relationship.

2. They wanted to be loved, cherished, and appreciated by the most important person in their lives—their man.

3. Their inability to be loved the way they wanted to be loved caused their frustration levels to go through the roof—even though many of them hid and masked that frustration from family and friends for years, even decades.

4. Even after terminal illness set in, many still did not receive the kind of love they desired.

5. Some died grasping for that which they would never receive.

Many of you make the same mistake; you love supremely hoping to get it in return. In fact, many of you love your husbands to death, literally! The way many of you function in your relationships, it will lead to a death—YOURS!

Many of you are placing your man on a pedestal, all the while failing to comprehend that if he doesn't automatically pull you up onto the pedestal with him, then it's safe to conclude that he doesn't realize that he should. If he doesn't realize he should return your love, then you increase the possibility, exponentially, of being on a collision course with marital issues, health issues, or both.

Women must be loved. They must—end of discussion. God knows that more than anyone. That is exactly why He commanded, "Husbands, love your wives, even as Christ also loved the church, and gave himself for it." (Ephesians 5:25)

There is no ambiguity here. It is not an option from God; it's a command! Men must love their women—period. The Creator knows the positive benefits that are experienced by a woman when she's loved by her man are immeasurable. God knows that a man's love is such a positive force in a woman's life that his love helps to insulate her body against disease! My favorite author, Ellen G. White, declares emphatically, "The husband should manifest great interest in his family.

Especially should he be very tender of the feelings of a feeble wife. HE CAN SHUT THE DOOR AGAINST MUCH DISEASE. Kind, cheerful and encouraging words will prove more effective than the most healing medicines."[5]

Be True to Yourself

In her book, *Woman's True Desire*, Danièle Starenkyj succinctly describes a woman's emotional response as "a woman who knows, who senses that she is not loved experiences a profound violation of her self, along with a pernicious anxiety. As if mired in a foul swamp, she vacillates, wishing for self-destruction, or the destruction of others. Not to be loved defies female logic. In her heart of hearts, she cannot comprehend it, tolerate it, or accept it. A woman who is unloved drinks day and night of bitter waters that make her dizzy and nauseous; plagued by migraines, nightmares, palpitations, hallucinations, hysteria, phobia and obsessions, her entire being seems to come unhinged. In short, woman's true desire is expressed in her absolute aversion to indifference."[6]

Brilliantly, Starenkyj adds that "[w]omen clamor to be loved: they refuse not to be loved. Can you hear them? Open your hearts and you will see them everywhere, appearing with a stubborn persistence impervious to the passage of time. Woman is defined by her need to be loved; it is a fundamental

---

5 Ellen G. White, *Adventist Home*, Review and Herald Publishing Association: Hagerstown, MD, p. 217.3

6 Danièle Starenkyj, *Women's True Desire*, Ulverton House Publications: Richmond, Quebec pp. 22, 23

need, immense and vital. It may be cultivated, suppressed, affected and corrupted, but it is absolute."[7]

Conversely, the Creator knows that when a woman is not loved, she becomes much more susceptible to illness and disease. Because women are such emotional beings, there are adverse consequences that impact a woman's body when she is not loved.

Sometimes those consequences are self-inflicted. We've all known women who, although in a committed relationship, were not happy for one reason or another. Rather than acquiesce and accept their fate, they fought for their marriage and family—and sometimes, that fight was literal if their men were cheating on them.

How many times has a woman gone to the other woman's house or job to confront her? How many times does that same woman get beaten by her man because she refuses to come to terms with his affair(s)? And the next time she's seen, her eyes are blackened and swollen as if they are badges of honor. No matter how many times he threatens her, she refuses to relent, because she refuses to share her man with another woman. She cannot because for a woman it is the violation of all violations. Her capacity to endure pain is legendary.

Starenkyj is correct when she says a woman refuses not to be loved. While they all don't go to this length, many are tenacious in their refusal to accept the hand their man has dealt them.

And, if an affair is the culprit and source of her unhappiness, she chomps down on it with hyena-like tenacity. It

---

7 Danièle Starenkyj, *Women's True Desire*, p. 23

consumes her. It depresses her. It debilitates her. And yet she wallows in it, incapable of walking away, letting it go, or moving on.

When forced to, she peppers him with questions about the most private details of the affair. Although the information locks her in a cell from which she may not soon be freed, she insists on torturing herself to the Nth degree. It's difficult to watch. It's painful to hear.

Unfortunately, women are being victimized by men on a daily basis all across America. The numbers are staggering. And yet there is no outcry. There is no dragnet to capture these perpetrators. There are no all-points bulletins to alert the American people as to their whereabouts. The victimizers are everywhere. They are in every city, every town, in every state in America, and ironically in EVERY CHURCH!

Strangely, women are their exclusive targets. The death toll of the women who have died is incalculable. An inordinate number of these women died with one common symptom—a broken heart.

The victimizers are husbands and boyfriends! They come from all walks of life. They range from politicians and police officers to pastors and pimps.

I will readily admit that while this is damning information, I submit to you that the mistreatment of the women in their lives, which is often the cause of the women's demise, is most often unintentional. However, the reality is tragic.

Don't Be a Victim

After 40 years of ministry, I've spoken to many of the women who would ultimately become victims. Some I've counseled; others I have watched from afar.

I've even reached out to many of their husbands and boyfriends in an attempt to save the relationship and, in so doing, save the life of the wife or girlfriend. Most often, I ran into a brick wall in an attempt to reach the man—notwithstanding that his wife/girlfriend already, in many cases, was suffering from a life-threatening illness as a result of existing in a toxic relationship that was sapping the very life from her body. Much more often than not, the man was not interested in counseling to resolve their issues. In fact, most of these men concluded that they were not going to be counseled by another man who they felt had their same issues. No matter how much his wife or girlfriend pleaded, no matter how much I appealed, those appeals, almost assuredly, fell on deaf ears.

As the brokenness continued unabated, invariably, I noticed a pattern. I discovered and later expected many of these women to experience health issues and problems. As I detected the level of frustration rising within her, I began to anticipate the onslaught of disease manifestations. And sure enough, consistently, I would be informed that the woman was now in a life-or-death struggle.

Now, not only did she have to deal with an unloving, unsympathetic man who seemed only to care for himself, but now she was also burdened with a life-threatening illness like cancer or a blood pressure that had run amuck, leading to frequent trips to the emergency room. Even with all of that, quite often, the man remained clueless to the fact that his failure to love his woman the way she desired was killing her.

Tragically, as you might expect, many of these cases don't end well for these women. They got weaker while the man's denial grew stronger.

More times than I care to remember, the woman fought gallantly to hold onto life but lost the battle, succumbed to her disease-riddled body, and died.

The cause of death, according to the death certificate, is something ominous like cancer, heart attack, stroke, etc. If we permit ourselves to be honest, we know better. The real cause of death: she died of a broken heart. All she wanted was for him to cherish and love her the way she loved him. All she wanted was for him to respect her. She merely wanted to spend time with him, go places and do things with him.

Honestly, I can't even imagine what it must feel like for these women who have sacrificed their lives for their men, waited on them hand and foot, served them morning, noon, and night, to contract a life-threatening illness, and yet their men still refuse to acknowledge that they need to make wholesale changes in their relationship with their women.

How do you give everything you have to a man, and then, when you need him to come through for you because you are now fighting to hold onto life, can he refuse to budge? How does that happen? In that scenario, that woman's pain and agony must be unbearable. The anger must be off the chain.

If I had my way, I'd rewrite the death certificate. It would read she died of a broken heart. She died loving a man who refused to love her the way she wanted and needed to be loved. She died in agony, desperately trying to make sense of the fact that she had given her all to a man who acted as if he couldn't care less.

If he doesn't love you, love yourself, take care of yourself, protect yourself. Do not accept or believe everything that comes out of the mouth of a man that doesn't have your best interest at heart. If all he does is put you down, criticize you, and complain that you don't do anything right—stop listening to that nonsense. For God's sake, stop believing everything he says about you. You know who you are. You know the kind of person you are. Never allow a man to rob you of your dignity and self-worth. He's not worth that—no man is. Protect your self-esteem at all costs. You are the only one who can. It is more precious to you than gold.

Too Close to Home

I found myself watching these beautiful women die in agony, getting mad at their husbands for being so selfish, so insensitive, so uncaring, so uncompassionate. And then, the unthinkable happened: my wife started experiencing a number of health-related problems. Either I didn't realize it at the time or chose not to, but I was the culprit.

Women can deal with a plethora of issues, but broken-heartedness is not on that list. When a woman is unhappy, unloved, disrespected, or cheated on, much more often than we realize, she becomes susceptible to illness and disease.

During the first seven years of marriage, when I was just a complete idiot, my wife was in and out of the hospital regularly.

Her blood pressure levels were through the roof consistently. She was rushed to the emergency room more times than I can count. After her blood pressure was stabilized or lowered later that day or the next, she'd be discharged. But the problem was that she'd always return to me and a toxic marriage, which was the root cause of her blood pressure issues.

In addition to being hospitalized because she was incapable of maintaining a healthy blood pressure, she was also hospitalized on a couple of occasions with pneumonia. While I am not a medical doctor, I know enough about health to understand that because of the toxic emotional waste that she was ingesting on a daily basis, primarily because she lived in a toxic waste dump called an unhealthy marriage, her immune system was compromised and ultimately incapable of warding off illness. Simply put, I was killing my wife slowly. And although that was not my intent, I was guilty, nevertheless.

It was approximately the seventh year of our marriage that I began to "get it." I made an about-face. I still didn't realize that I should love her the way she wanted to be loved (my eyes would not be opened to that revelation for a few more years), but I knew that I could no longer love her the way that I had. Needless to say, when Angela and I started attending The Voice In The Wilderness Mission, and we sat at the feet of Vernon and Sheree Dawson and listened intently to their presentations on the effect that a broken heart and spirit has on a woman, it was indeed an eye opener. I knew that I was killing the woman that I pledged to love, cherish, and care for "till death do us part."

But knowing that I was killing her because of my actions and behaviors was only part of the solution. The main problem was that I didn't know how to love her the way she wanted to be loved. And ladies, now I realize that is the key to marital and relational happiness. I didn't want her to die from a stroke or heart attack. I didn't want to lose her. It's just that I didn't know how to love her.

So, guess what I did? I began to pray. In my prayers I asked God to teach me how to be a good husband. I asked him to teach me how to be loving, kind, sensitive, and compassionate to my wife. I asked him to teach me how to love her the way she wanted to be loved. I knew that if I could do that, then Angela would indeed be happy because the happiness would be on her terms and not mine.

I was honest and sincere in my prayers. I admitted my faults and wrongdoing. I acknowledged the damage that I had done in my marriage. I asked Him to help me make the necessary changes before I ran my wife away permanently. I divulged that I was incapable of doing this on my own—that without His help, I knew that I was headed for divorce and another failed marriage. And worse yet, I knew that my wife's health was worsening, and I understood that I was the culprit. She was suffering because of me. This was a battle I had to win, and I knew it. Therefore, I prayed without ceasing. I'm happy to announce that an incredible thing happened: God heard my prayers.

My Mission

Far too many women are getting sick and eventually dying because they are not being loved the way they want to be loved. Something must be done about it. I cannot stand idly by and watch it anymore. I must speak up. I must do more. I am doing more.

I get it now. Typically, when I counsel couples, it's because the woman has sought out my help. Almost always, it's the woman who's unhappy but is desperately trying to save the relationship. If I can get through to the man, I can begin to help him with the process of loving his wife the way she wants to be loved. I try to make it clear that if he does, the relationship will turn the corner. I explain that he will get what he wants when she gets what she wants. It's incredible how much of a game-changer this concept is. When BOTH parties are happy, the relationship is healthy.

But unfortunately, often I am forced to work with women alone because it's difficult to get men to attend counseling sessions on an ongoing, consistent basis. Because of his absence, I have one objective—to teach each woman how to teach her man to love her the way she wants to be loved. During my seminars, and particularly the "90 Days To Identify & Mesmerize the Man of Your Dreams" group coaching sessions, I provide women with the tools to get what they need in their relationships to be happy.

I make it clear that it is not selfish to want your needs met. Let's face it—if your man is the happiest man on the planet, but you're miserable because he's not attentive to meeting and fulfilling your needs, then you cannot and will not be happy in that scenario.

I have drawn my line in the sand to provide you with the help you need. I hope it's good enough. I hope it's soon enough.

Action Plan
FOR CHAPTER 2

I want you to reflect on your own situation and consider ways in which you will stand up for yourself, take your mental and physical health seriously, and own the power you have as a woman. Listen to me carefully because many women have a problem with focusing on themselves as if it is a sin. It is not. There is nothing selfish about this. Everybody and everything can't come before your needs. You must fight for you because if you don't, no one else will!

1. Read the book *Woman's True Desire* by Danièle Starenkyj. It will be a game-changer for you. You must establish a new standard as to how you will be treated by the man in your life. Even if he's your husband, he needs to learn to love you on your terms, not his! You must insist on this. Your happiness depends on it.

2. Discover exactly HOW you want your man to treat you. You must determine what is and what is not acceptable behavior from him. Therefore, I suggest that you make a list entitled "Loving Me The Way I Want To Be Loved." The list will have two parts.

Part one: "My Husband/Boyfriend Will." In this section you will clearly indicate the way in which you want to be treated. Here's the deal: if he loves or cares for you, then he should want to fulfill every item on your list, as long as the list is reasonable.

Part two: "My Husband/Boyfriend Will Not…" or "My Husband/Boyfriend Will Stop…" This one is self-explanatory.

3. Consider your approach. I want you to know that, as it relates to implementing this process, approach is everything. Your approach must be flawless. You cannot nag him into submission; you must draw him into changing his behavior. You cannot approach him with attitude and start demanding. You will fail!

Pick your time and place. Always take him up before you take him down. For example, start the conversation by telling him how much you love him. Extol his good points. After having made him feel good about himself, transition to the pain point you want to discuss. You might say something like, "but there is something that is bothering me that we need to discuss." You must always stay a couple steps ahead of him. Think things through carefully. Lead with your brainpower.

4. Draw a line in the sand on this one NOW! Pray. Ask God to provide you with all the information that you need to teach your man to love you on your terms. No matter how long you've been together, no matter how unhappy you've been or how impossible this might seem, many, if not most of you, can teach your man to love you the way you want to be loved and not the way he wants to love you. The longevity of your relationship, but, more importantly, your quality of life could depend on it. So, stop playing Russian roulette with it!

5. Enroll in "90 Days to Identify & Mesmerize the Man of Your Dreams" group coaching sessions to master the art of getting your man to love you on your terms! (Consult my website: www.theartofwomanhood.org)

Ladies, no matter how insensitive and clueless he appears to be, with the mercy and grace of God, he can change. I'm a living witness. My wife required me to change without raising her voice.

She said, "If you are going to be my husband, this is how you are going to treat me." And most importantly, she meant it. She knew what she wanted, and she insisted on getting it. I became a changed husband as a result.

CHAPTER 3

THE TRUE MEANING OF HELPMEET

God's Purpose

First and foremost, let's set the record straight. God's plan was that a woman would be happy, fulfilled, self-actualized, and most importantly, empowered.

It is the express reason that God took Eve from a rib from Adam's side. This act indicated that Eve (who represented all women) was to be equal in status with Adam (who represented all men).

What many people fail to understand is that God is about equity and fairness. God is not imbalanced. He is not misogynistic. To prove that, He made Eve equal in status with Adam from the very beginning.

Women were designed, by the creator, to wield tremendous influence in their relationships with their men.

It has never been God's plan for them to function as wimps and doormats to their husbands or men in general. They were intended to wield Godly power and influence for the purpose of fulfilling His objective.

God created women with brilliant minds and outstanding reasoning abilities. He gave women an intuition that men do not possess. When a man follows and heeds his woman's intuition, it safeguards and insulates the relationship, the marriage, and the family against would-be disaster. In short, husbands should listen to their wives. We would all be much better off if we did.

That notwithstanding, in my experience with the women that I work with in my coaching program, I have come to the conclusion that most women fail to realize the power that they possess because, as one who regularly works with women, it's my observation that most women have yet to discover their God-appointed mission in life.

It is my experience that the average woman has no idea of one of the most important roles and functions that God has called them to. Because they are unaware of what their purpose is, they are incapable of fulfilling that task to the best of their ability. I shall attempt, in my feeble way, to shed light on that high and noble calling that God has extended to women, especially wives.

As we would suspect, there are obstacles and barriers designed to forever prevent women from reaching their full potential.

The culprits are varied. Satan, whose hatred of women is unquestioned, has adversely influenced society at large—and even some religious organizations—to prevent women from successfully accomplishing their God-ordained objective, which is to "help" their husbands/men be the best they can be for God, their families, and society as a whole.

To prevent that eventuality and to minimize a woman's influence over her man, whenever and wherever possible, Satan relegated women to second- and third-class citizenship.

We've all seen the images or the newscasts of how women have been treated over the millennia. Most recently, we've come to watch in horror the impact that Sharia Law in the Islamic world in some, not all, Islamic nations, has on the denigration of women. We've seen how poorly women have been, and still are being, treated in Afghanistan at the hands of the Taliban. We've read about women in India who are ignited with gasoline and burned to death by their husbands who no longer desire them. We've cringed at the knowledge of young African girls who are mutilated to prevent them from being promiscuous.

However, none, I repeat, none of this is God's will. It is not consistent with God's plan for women emanating from Genesis 2 detailing the Garden of Eden experience, which functions and serves as the blueprint for how we should pattern our lives.

God's purpose for women was high and noble. Genesis 2:18 is the clue to unlocking the power and influence that God intended for all women to wield in their relationships with men—and that power is substantive.

Genesis 2:18 says, "And the Lord God said, It is not good that the man should be alone; I will make a helpmeet for him." This Gen. 2:18 principle, as I refer to it, is pregnant with implications for women.

The best gift, after Jesus Christ and the Holy Ghost, that God gave to mankind was a woman. Moreover, when God placed women in men's lives, He imbued them with awesome gifts and tremendous influence so that women would help men be the best that they can be for the Lord.

As a helpmeet, your responsibility is to use all the gifts and talents in your arsenal in your quest to help the man in your life be all that God would have him be. Make no mistake about it, no one can help him accomplish this like you can—no one. Neither his parents, siblings, coworkers, nor friends are capable of helping him to be what God has called him to be. You are the most influential and only indispensable person in his life, barring none.

You have the uncanny and unrivaled ability to make your man believe that the sky is the limit. When you look him in his eyes and inform him that he can be anything he wants to be, when you convince him that he can start his own business or go back to school, he believes it. When you inform him that he has what it takes to become the next Barack Obama and there is nothing that he cannot accomplish by the grace of God, not only does he believe it, but he'll break his neck trying to prove you right.

Because you have put him on such a pedestal and believe in him so much, he will refuse to disappoint you. Therefore, he will work his fingers to the bone. He will work two and three jobs.

Why? It's really simple. Understand the dynamic that's going on here. The Almighty determined that because of the Gen. 2:18 principle, a woman would establish a standard for her man to strive for. She would visualize and verbalize where she thinks he should be in life. She places the bar high and believes with every fiber in her being that he can attain such lofty heights.

Because of his love for his wife, her vision becomes his vision. Her standard becomes his standard. Because of her confidence in him, he is driven to excellence.

When you say he can go through a brick wall, he believes it. It's simply that you've established goals and objectives for him to strive for.

What a Difference She Can Make

Case in point, while I was a student in the seminary, my wife at the time said to me over and over again that, according to all our friends, "You are the smartest student in the seminary." When I asked her if she agreed with that notion, she declared emphatically, "Yes!" That one simple statement drove me more than you can imagine. Because we were poor students and I couldn't give her the kind of material things that I knew she desired and deserved, I gave her the one thing that I could—pride. My goal in life was to make her proud of me by studying hard and being at the top of my class.

It was for that reason that my wife and children, on several occasions, went to bed at night while I remained at the kitchen table studying. The next morning when they arose, I was still at the kitchen table studying for a Hebrew or Akkadian final exam. Make no mistake about it: it was her belief in me that became the driving force in my life.

I concluded that if she was going to have that much confidence in me, then the least I could do was to work hard to be worthy of such confidence.

And work hard I did. I was driven to become the best theologian, not just in the Seventh-day Adventist Church, but in the world.

I swallowed the bait hook, line, and sinker. She had provided me with the impetus to excel and not just get by. She single-handedly provided the motivation to never settle for second-best. She helped forge my identity as an excellent student, budding theologian, entrepreneur, and businessman, etc.

I can honestly admit that she has much to do with the person I am today. Her imprint is all over me because those seeds were planted during the years we were together. Even though the marriage did not last, she had a profound effect on the man I've become.

Fast-forward several years. I had returned home from Michigan because the Adventist seminary I was attending refused to admit me into their Ph.D. program, even though I had already demonstrated during the completion of my master's program that I was qualified to do scholarly work, when my wife decided she no longer wanted to be married.

She ran off with some dude at her job. She left me with the children, who I gladly raised with the help of my family and inner circle of friends.

I was completely blindsided by this turn of events. I was completely unprepared for the prospect of going through life alone—with young children no less. I was wiped out. I never contemplated going through life without my wife and the mother of my children being on my arm. My pain was greater than I can even explain. It was like the sky was falling, and I couldn't stop it.

In public I played the role of the strong man to perfection, but when home, alone, I was a sniveling mess. In private I cried repeatedly, as if that would bring her back.

I had a temp job at Educational Testing Services in Princeton, New Jersey. I thought I was doing well. I assumed that it would ultimately turn into a long-term assignment. I was wrong. I rushed into work one day only to be informed that my services were no longer needed, that my assignment had, in fact, expired. I was devastated. I couldn't handle it. Here it was again—that dreaded "R" word—rejection.

So how did I respond? You guessed it. I cried. I went home, fell on the couch, and drowned myself in my sorrows. "Why is this happening to me?" I asked myself repeatedly.

Then it happened. I called my best friend Katie Mendenhall. Katie was my lifeline. Katie was my rock. Katie and I were inseparable.

I never would have made it through the darkest time in my life had it not been for the best friend that any human being could have. She single-handedly saved me because she categorically refused to allow me to give up and wallow in my tears and accept this temporary setback as a permanent defeat.

Without either one of us knowing it, she implemented the Gen. 2:18 principle that day. More than riches untold, it was, without a doubt, the best gift she could have ever given me that day.

I told Katie, while fighting back the tears on the phone, that I had been let go from my job.

Without hesitation, she declared, "I'll be right over." When she came in and saw me still wallowing in self-pity, she authoritatively said, "Get up. I will not let you fail. You are the smartest man I know. Now get up."

Is there any doubt in your mind that I obeyed? There shouldn't be. I didn't have a choice. She erected a standard for me. She painted a picture for me, a picture that had been obscured in my eyes because of my pain. But that picture was crystal clear in hers.

I couldn't see what she saw. I was blindsided by hurt, pain, disappointment, self-pity, and apparent failure. I needed to lean on someone and borrow their picture because, at the time, I didn't have one. Katie was the person I leaned on. I couldn't have made a better choice.

She believed in me. She was convinced that I was going somewhere in life. And because I was her best friend, she absolutely refused to allow me to live down to my failures and pain instead of rising to my abilities. She insisted that I rise to her expectations.

She became my eyes because I was blind. She became my compass because I was lost. She was my rudder when my ship was hopelessly adrift at sea being buffeted by the winds of trial and the vicissitudes of life.

By the sheer force of her personality, and because she knew that this was just a temporary setback for me, she became my tower of power and my driving force.

And then, she did it again.

I was headed to prayer meeting one Wednesday evening. As I was driving to church, inexplicably, the devil began to mess with me. He began telling me that my life was a complete failure. Worse yet, he suggested that I should commit suicide, for I had nothing to live for. When I remonstrated with him that I had to go on living for my children, who were 12 and 10 at the time, he dismissed even that notion by suggesting that my parents and family would easily take my place.

While on the way to the House of God, I suddenly found myself in this life-and-death struggle with the enemy of my soul, and I was losing. Because I was already feeling like I was a complete failure and had let everyone down, I had very little ammunition to fight back.

I was distraught. Correction, I was suicidal. Sitting in the office of my very first church assignment, in the dark, I fought for a reason to live, and I couldn't come up with one—NOT EVEN ONE!

I was desperate. The tears were flowing. I was losing it. I didn't know where to turn. I didn't know what to do. I felt like I was on this huge sliding board. I was sliding into hell and death, and there was absolutely nothing that I could do to stop it.

The saddest part about all of this is that for about 20 minutes, he had me. I can't even explain why I, the most confident person I knew, would embrace that nonsense. As I sat in my office feeling like the hourglass had been turned upside down on me and that I was rapidly running out of time, I looked at the clock. It was 7:10 p.m., and no one had arrived for the prayer meeting yet. It was then that the thought popped into my head. Without hesitating, I ran out the door, hoped in my car, and drove straight to Katie's job.

Because that was 1985, I can't tell you what words she employed to get me back up on my feet again. But I do remember that when she was finished, I was back on the pedestal; my confidence was back. I had many reasons to go on living, and live I did, which is why I'm able to share a story that I've never told before—not even to my wife to this very day.

Don't get it twisted. This is not about Satan's power to overwhelm God's people when they hit rock bottom and are incapable of fighting back. No, this is about a woman's ability to do for a man that which very few men could have been able to replicate in that moment with my life seemingly hanging in the balance.

I am convinced that no one else on planet earth could have ministered to me so effectively as a woman that day. Thank God for the Gen. 2:18 principle and my best friend, Katie.

Katie, if you are reading this, I want you to know that I love you, and I will be forever indebted to you for picking me up, dusting me off, and starting me on my life's journey again. Although at times it seemed that I was not imbibing each day's life lesson that you were imparting because I was so entrenched in my pain, I want you to know that I heard every word of wisdom that fell like precious crumbs to a starving man from your lips. I am truly proud to admit that you were my teacher, and I was your willing student.

Woman's Ultimate Power

I could never adequately repay Katie for what she did for my family, but most importantly me. She taught me valuable lessons that summer. One of the most important things I learned from my friend was the all-important concept that there are some women who masterfully teach their men how to love them without them knowing they're being taught. Katie taught me that lesson, and I've never forgotten it. And now, several decades later, I, who once was the student of a woman, have become the teacher of this same awesome concept to other women.

Now, let's fast-forward to 1991 when I met my Angela, who, a year later, became my wife. I didn't know it at the time, but I was an absolute mess when we met: residual effects from a previously failed marriage, a broken heart, and just plain ole not truly converted.

The first seven years of our marriage were pure hell. I accept all the blame. I was convinced that I had made a mistake, and I was going to correct it. Divorce was a foregone conclusion—it was a when and not an if.

Then that thing showed up again—the Gen. 2:18 principle. You see, I was convinced that the problems in our marriage were all her fault. However, she was having none of it. Right around this time, as I was deeply involved in the blame game, she said something that would change the course of my life forever.

We were riding home from the Film & TV Workshops in Rockport, Maine. It was a 10-hour trip home. Obviously, we had lots of time on our hands.

In the midst of our conversation, she challenged me to be the priest of our home. She challenged me that if I led, she would follow. She challenged me to be the head of my home. In essence, even though I'm sure she didn't know what she was doing at the time, she challenged my manhood!

Wait a minute. No one challenged my manhood without me stepping up to the plate to answer that challenge. I had to respond positively.

See, I was raised by a mother and a manly man as a father. He modeled manhood to me. I grew up with a picture in my head, for the most part, of how a man is supposed to act and behave.

Therefore, I considered myself a man. When Angela called that into question, I had no other recourse but to rise to the occasion. She questioned whether I could be that guy. She raised the bar on me. She erected a standard of leadership that she expected me to fulfill. There was no ambivalence concerning the picture that was firmly entrenched in her brain as to how she expected me to function.

She expected me to lead. She required me to lead. She put the onus squarely on me. It was now put up or shut up.

I had promised God that I would not walk away until I could honestly say that I had done everything in my power to save the marriage. I knew that at that point, I could not make that declaration. Therefore, I had some work to do.

We both pledged that divorce was not an option. Once divorce was taken off the table, we were left with just one other option—happiness.

I realized that I was incapable of loving Angela the way she wanted to be loved because I erroneously expected her to meet my every need with minimal effort on my part to meet hers. Ladies, that's not Biblical. That's backwards.

I had to show what I was made of. This was no time to wimp out now. Because of the picture that she had of what a real godly man was like, I was challenged to be that and then some.

I chose to accept that challenge. I chose to be the godly head of my home, husband, father, priest, provider, protector, and burden-bearer she expected me to be.

Consequently, I assumed the responsibility for the deplorable state of our marriage. It was on me. "If you lead, I will follow" kept ringing in my ears. I decided to lead the way God intended me to lead.

We remained together for the next 22 years until she passed September 3, 2021, of COVID-19, after 29 years of marriage.

That is not the full extent of her influence, however. I shamefully admit that when we married over 20 years ago, I was a deeply flawed individual. I masked my imperfections. But I could not hide them from her.

One of my problems was that I was hopelessly addicted to pornography. The worst part about it was that I expected her to indulge with me. Somewhere along the way, I must have bumped my head—hard!

One just needs to have known my wife to realize how foolish I had to be to even consider the notion of the two of us watching porn together. My wife was serious about her relationship with God. She bled Seventh-day Adventism. It's all she knew. It's what she believed in. It wasn't just her religion. It was her way of life. She didn't want to be anything else. And more importantly, she was not about to allow me to cause her to compromise her beliefs and convictions.

She said to me, "You will not bring that stuff in my house." I made twice as much money as she did, but she called it her house, and she meant it.

The message was unambiguous. It was clear, absolutely, positively, categorically, without hesitation or equivocation, that "filth" was not coming in her house! I find it amazing that every cotton-pickin' thing in my house belonged to my wife, even if I bought it.

And in case I hadn't gotten it the first time, she made the appeal personal. She reminded me that I was the man of God. How in the world could I stand before God's people and exhort them to righteousness, and yet live a double life?

She called me on the carpet. She called my actions hypocrisy. She was right, even though I didn't readily comply. All I can say is that sin makes you stupid. Sin blinds you and makes wrong right and right wrong.

But because of her perseverance and her convictions, I became convicted. Because of her standard of holiness, I began to desire holiness.

After tiring of being on a roller-coaster ride in my quest for moral purity, after repeatedly failing to achieve victory over this addiction, I felt I had no other recourse than to go into the pulpit and expose myself and my struggle to my members one Sabbath morning and ask the people of God to pray for me.

I have come completely out of the closet as it relates to my past porn addiction. I am clean. It's by no means easy. Temptation lies behind every door.

Don't miss the point here. It was my wife's standards that I felt compelled to live up to. She established the godly standard that I now strive to live up to at all times. She became my standard-bearer until I was able to establish my own standard of righteousness.

Her imprint on my life is unmistakable. I am the man I am today because of my wife. I have the relationship that I have with God because of my wife. I am a much better person and pastor because she required me to be the best I could be and because she refused to accept anything less than my best.

Other Women of Strength

Now, does this principle apply to the mother/son relationship, or is it mutually exclusive to the husband/wife relationship? It applies equally to both. Permit me to explain.

Ora Legette, my mother, has been the driving force in my life since the day I was born. She has lauded me for my intelligence. She consistently says to me, "Legette, if I had your brains, I'd be a millionaire." I believe her. My mom is simply amazing.

For years now, she's had a standard of success that she expects me to achieve. And, because she believes that I can achieve that level of success, she refuses to allow me to be comfortable where I am. She's constantly pushing me to achieve the greatness that she feels I'm capable of realizing.

She has a picture in her head of where she feels I should be. She will go to her grave gently nudging me in the direction she's convinced I should be headed. Because of her internal picture of how she sees me, she feels I should have arrived at a certain level of success already. And, as long as my life does not harmonize with that picture, she will gently encourage me to kick it in gear.

But most importantly, she has chastised me for not applying myself and writing the books that she knew I should have written long ago.

Mom constantly says to me, "Son, I'm getting older now. I want to see your name on a book. I want to see your films, before I die." She regularly says, "Son, I want you to finish your Ph.D. before I close my eyes."

Continuously, I hear these words ringing in my ears. Her vision for my life is ever present. It is another driving force toward my future.

And you know what? I'm going back to school to finish my doctoral degree because that's what my mom wants and expects of me. That's the Gen. 2:18 principle at its best.

Permit me to demonstrate how powerful this principle is. My mother passed away November 21, 2022 at the ripe old age of 89. Even though she's in the grave awaiting the resurrection, she is still one of the major driving forces of my life. Moreover, she always will be.

Speaking of a driving force, I dare not forget my aunts, Henrietta Mason and Betty Redd. It was Aunt Henrietta who first envisioned me as an evangelist/pastor when that concept was the farthest thing from my mind.

Both Aunt Henrietta and Aunt Betty saw something in me and began pushing me towards Oakwood College (now Oakwood University). They weren't relentless, but they were consistent.

Aunt Henrietta, in particular, kept planting seeds until the notion of being a preacher started to germinate in my brain and I began to give it serious thought and consideration.

She saw before I did. She knew it before I ever contemplated it. She was convinced I had it in me. But more importantly, she was convinced that it was God's will for my life. Consequently, she felt justified in pushing me in the direction that she was convinced God was leading me.

And finally, there is Ebelin Rolen. She is an absolute Godsend for me. She pushes me. She encourages me to excel. She playfully threatens me to finish my projects because women need the information that God has so graciously shared with me. She challenges me to focus and not be distracted. Because she believes in me wholeheartedly, she refuses to permit me to settle for second-best.

I am almost afraid to disappoint her because she believes in me about as much as I believe in myself. Every man needs a woman like Ebelin Rolen. Every man needs someone like her who not only pushes them to be the absolute best that they can be but insists on it! For the men who are fortunate to have been blessed with an Ebelin Rolen in their lives, they are destined for certain greatness if they are wise enough to listen to her sage counsel.

There are no words in the King's English to describe how blessed I am to have her in my life. I don't know what I would do if she, and her incredible husband, Jeff, were not a part of my inner circle and two of the best friends I've ever had in life. But I can assure you of one thing: under no circumstances do I want to find out.

All of these women have been the difference-makers throughout my lifetime. They have shaped and molded me into the man I am today. Their positive influence predetermined the direction of my life and prevented me from veering off course.

I shudder to think where I would be today if they had not had such a profound impact on my life. The thought is downright scary.

Own Your Influence

Continuing on the subject of a woman's influence in a man's life, do you really think that Barack Hussein Obama would have become the first African American president in the history of these United States of America without the presence of a very strong woman by his side?

I am convinced that there would never have been a President Barack without a First Lady Michelle—never! And that is not to take away from the President's super intelligence, talent, charisma, and destiny.

But what it does is reflect the kind of power and influence that God intended women to wield. God wants women to know that they are the driving force in men's lives. You alone are your man's catalyst. Ladies, your men may be the ship, but you are the rudder. He may be the boat, but you are truly the sail. Yes, he may be the plane, but you are the altimeter—and you help determine his altitude!

The Almighty would have you know that with you by your man's side, he can achieve anything.

I shared my experience because I want you to know that because of you, he can reach the unreachable, dream the impossible, accomplish the unattainable, achieve the unthinkable, and attempt the unimaginable.

I hope and pray that upon reading this book you will realize how valuable you are—period! Your husband may never tell you. Your children may not realize that they need to verbalize it to you, and your grandchildren and great-grandchildren may be too self-absorbed to give it a second thought. But I want you to know that you are the apple of God's eye. I want you to realize that this world could never function for a nanosecond without YOU.

If every woman on the planet took a vacation to another planet for 24 hours, there would be one hue and cry collectively from virtually every husband on the planet that goes like this, "Honey, where are my socks?"

It doesn't matter what your experience has been—you're still the best gift that God could have given to a man. Some of you have had to overcome horrific odds in your lifetime, and yet you're still an incredible woman. Some of you have been physically, sexually, verbally, or emotionally abused by husbands and boyfriends, and yet many of you go on to become these incredibly gifted professionals. I don't know how you do it.

Over the ages, men have harmed you every way imaginable. Some men should have been arrested and imprisoned for failing to treat you as God would have had them do. And even though some of the men in your lives have been veritable monsters, you've loved them, nevertheless. I truly don't understand that kind of love. I say this unabashedly: most men do not deserve to have you by their sides.

But no matter what mistakes men have made and perpetrated towards you over the millennia, God's purpose for you is crystal clear: He wants you to experience true happiness in this lifetime. And because most of you are the marrying kind, God also wants that for you, your spouse, and your children.

However, if you hope to experience true, lasting happiness within your marriage or relationship, it is imperative that you, like the women above, master this Gen. 2:18 principle. When you help your man become everything God has destined for him to be for his family, and when you assist him in fulfilling his God-given roles that he alone cannot accomplish, you safeguard your family from dangerous threats—seen and unseen, known and unknown.

One of the threats that is ravaging the human family today, running roughshod through household after household, is the phenomenon of men failing to understand their roles as the heads of their homes. It's having dire consequences on families and relationships.

But before you proceed, I need you to listen to me carefully. You are, without a shadow of a doubt, the most powerful individual on Planet Earth. You have the juice; you have the power. If you don't think so, put this book down right now and read two chapters in the Bible. They will demonstrate one thing clearly: when you take a woman who has mastered her God-given gifts and you pit her against either the strongest man in the world or the most powerful man in the world, it's not even close. For the woman who has mastered the wonderful art of womanhood, it's like taking candy from a baby. So, put this book down and pick up your Bible. Read these two chapters: 1 Samuel 25 and Judges 16. Resume this chapter once you're done.

Done? See what I mean? The two powerful men in those stories never had a chance. One woman inspired her man to do good, while the other woman chose to inspire her man to do evil. Both, however, inspired their men to action using their giftedness.

Why were those women so incredibly powerful? It's because they mastered the art of womanhood. If you implement the techniques that I teach either in this book or my coaching program, you too, like these awesome women, will become a power broker—hopefully for good.

Action Plan

FOR CHAPTER 3

After reading this chapter and the stories I shared, here are some steps you can take to apply these concepts to your own life:

1. Understand that you are the best thing that could ever happen to a man, after God of course. Therefore, you must know your value and your place in his life. When you realize how valuable you are in God's sight first and foremost, then it should help you to see how precious you are to everyone else—including a man. Once you realize your worth, there are certain things you should not tolerate, particularly men who will not love you the way you want and need to be loved.

2. Master the Gen. 2:18 principle. You must erect a standard for your man to adhere to, strive for, and live up to. YOU must do that for him. Please understand that it's your role to help him be the best that he can be. No one on earth can help him attain such lofty heights as you. Please understand that you are indispensable. You have power and influence in his life. Use it for good.

CHAPTER 4

"YOU JUST DON'T GET IT, DO YOU?"

Ignorance of a Young Man

"Pastor, he just doesn't get it."

If I had a dollar for every time a woman has levied that charge against her man, I'd have a hefty bank account. I've heard it from women of all ages. Unfortunately, this same charge has been levied against me—several times. And the worst part about it is that I deserved it. I didn't get it either. Permit me to share my story.

I married Beverly right out of high school. We attended junior high school together. We were in the same homeroom in seventh grade. For the three years that we attended Grice Junior High in Hamilton, New Jersey, neither of us were attracted to each other. But that rapidly changed when we started high school at Hamilton High West. As sophomores, we had a math class together at the start of our sophomore year, during fifth period, the next-to-last period of the day. We sat at the back of the class overlooking the courtyard below.

We played checkers to pass the time. She beat me badly day after day. Each day, I came to class with the determination that that was the day I was finally going to turn the tide and win one game. Can't a brother win just one game?

We played, we laughed, we joked, we talked, and we got to know each other. We had never spent such intimate time with each other before. I guess it was timing.

I could feel something happening. Something was growing between us with each passing day even though I tried to deny it because I already had a girlfriend that I was committed to.

Somehow, I had developed the mindset that cheating was not cool. Maybe it was because of my strict Seventh-day Adventist upbringing. Or maybe it was because my mom prided herself on being a one-man woman. Therefore, I developed a similar concept. I'm not sure what it was. All I know is that I tried to put the brakes on it but to no avail.

There was something different about Bev. I know what it was: it was her laugh. Girlfriend had such a hearty laugh that it was sexy. It was appealing. I was irresistibly drawn to her.

I tried to withstand her charms, but I was powerless to resist. I never shall forget the day. I was 15, and we were driving around in a stolen car. We drove by a friend's house, and there she was. I got out of the car. When she spotted me, she turned and began walking in my direction.

It was as if time stood still. She sauntered—yes, that's the right word—up to me, as if in super S-L-O-W M-O-T-I-O-N. She came and stood right in front of me, almost nose to nose, and looked me in the eyes. I was breathing heavily. I started sweating. Watching her walk towards me, I was thinking, "Oh my gosh, I'm going to pass out."

It's funny as I look back on those days. It's clear to me now that Bev had mastered the art of being a flower at the tender age of 15! Her ability to mesmerize and draw was uncanny for a young lady her age.

I knew I was smitten when I found myself at home, in my room, lying on my back, looking up at the ceiling and picturing her raucous laugh.

I know, I know, I was only 15 years old, but no young lady made me feel like Bev made me feel. She arrested my thoughts. She incarcerated my heart.

I had to have her. And there was no doubt in my mind that I would, notwithstanding that she had a boyfriend, Robert. That was of no consequence to me. Why? Because I thought I was the man.

I had a history of pursuing girls who had boyfriends, and when they fell in love with me, I moved on because the thrill was now gone. So, I thought it would be a breeze. It wasn't. For the first time, I lost at love.

Fast-forward to August 1970. It was several weeks prior to the start of our senior year. I didn't realize it at the time, but I made the single most important decision of my life.

I concluded that the #1 objective I wanted to fulfill my senior year was not to be the starting defensive back on my high school football team—even though I was. My #1 objective was not to win a varsity letter in football, get my varsity jacket, and make the all-city team as one of the best defensive backs in Mercer County, New Jersey—which I did. My #1 objective was not to get my license, run indoor and spring track—which I did as well. My #1 objective was not even to graduate the following June—which I did.

I came into the year knowing that before the school year ended, Beverly Webb had to be my girlfriend prior to graduation. I knew that if we graduated and she was with him, they were going to get married, and I'd miss out on the woman that I knew I wanted to spend the rest of my life with.

Did I mention that I was 16?

No one had ever made me work so hard. I now know that was one of the reasons I was so drawn to her. Fortunately for me, my dreams came true. On April 23, 1971, after having my patience and loved tested, I asked her to be my girlfriend while sitting in my car in front of my house. She said "yes," and we became official. I knew then and there that she would be my wife and life's partner. I knew it.

One year later on July 29th, 1972, we were joined together in holy matrimony. I was on cloud nine. She was an excellent wife and mother. She was everything I hoped for in a woman. On top of that, we eventually had two wonderful children.

Although growing up Baptist, what made the deal even sweeter is that she embraced my faith—the Seventh-day Adventist Church. We were on the same page spiritually.

In addition to that, we both attended Oakwood University and Andrews University, and we fulfilled our educational dreams simultaneously. I received my bachelor's and master's degrees while she completed her bachelor's degree. I couldn't have been happier.

I thought we were in for the long haul. I really thought it would be "till death do us part." You couldn't have convinced me otherwise. All through college and graduate school, we were lauded as the "perfect couple" by our friends.

In fact, we were often sought out by classmates who were contemplating marriage. It was a match made in heaven, or so I thought, until she came home from work early that Sunday, September 2nd, 1984, and declared, "I don't love you, and I don't think I want to spend the rest of my life with you."

I turned and looked around the room, wandering if she were talking to someone else besides me, even though we were alone.

I turned to her and said, "Who are you talking to because I know you're not talking to me?"

Little did I know it at the time, but my marriage was over. I discovered that she was terribly unhappy. She accused me of not getting it.

I retorted, "What don't I get? What am I not doing? Tell me so I can fix it."

She was adamant. She was not willing to tell me because she was convinced that I should have known. She declared that with all my education, I needed to pull out some of my books and figure out what the problem was and fix it without her assistance.

For the life of me, I didn't know what the problem was. I was completely confused. She waited on me hand and foot. I was the king of her castle. I was floored because I couldn't have been happier. All my needs were being met—all of them. For the longest time, I thought her needs were being met as well. Boy, was I wrong.

The problem was that her frustration quotient had soared to dangerous levels without my knowledge. She later revealed

I was incapable of changing. The recurring picture that commandeered her brain was one of perpetual unhappiness. She pictured me as a self-absorbed boy who was stuck in his ways rather than a mature, selfless man who placed her needs before my own. And rather than remain tethered to a sinking ship, she opted to bail out of the marriage.

I was devastated. I was blindsided. I never saw it coming. I'm now convinced that I should have. I realize that my own flaws and failures blinded me to her needs because I was too focused on myself. The marriage ended after 14 years, when it should have lasted "till death do us part" had it not been for the fact that I really didn't get it.

I ruined a good marriage. I wrecked a wonderful relationship because I thought the solar system revolved around me. I subjected my children to hurt and pain that is felt to this day—over four decades later. My family fell apart because I was so into myself that I failed to see that she was hurting and crying out to be loved the way she wanted and deserved to be loved.

All she wanted was for me to give her what she was giving me. All she wanted was some tender loving kindness, some thoughtfulness every now and then. All she wanted was a flower, a card, a gift even though it wasn't her birthday or our anniversary. She merely wanted me to make a statement to her that I loved her as much as she loved me, but I didn't do that. Honestly, I was incapable of doing that because I was too busy requiring her to love me as I marinated in her love.

In short, I didn't know how to love Bev the way she wanted to be loved. I didn't know how to meet her needs or put her on a pedestal, which is where she had placed me. I didn't know how to reciprocate. And the saddest part of all is I really didn't realize that I didn't know how to. Or, worse yet, I didn't realize that I needed to.

Demand Your Happiness

There was one major mistake that Bev made, even though neither of us realized it at the time. I now know that most of the women who attend my course to learn how to achieve the love they desire and deserve are guilty of the same. The problem was that she never verbally required me to reciprocate. If she had only voiced her unhappiness, thrown a temper tantrum, fussed me out, something to show how miserable she was, I would have gotten the message and kicked it in gear—I would have. But she was content with showering me with love, pleasing me, and waiting on me hand and foot. In fact, I can't tell you the number of times she declared to me how much she enjoyed spoiling me.

That was the picture she grew up watching at home as she observed how her mother took care of her father. It came naturally to Bev. She did it so well that I erroneously assumed that I didn't have to respond in kind. I guess I honestly thought that she derived such pleasure out of loving, spoiling, and pampering me that she didn't require me to love her similarly. So, I didn't. I allowed her to love me supremely, to give to me incessantly, and to sacrifice for me daily.

But the problem with this scenario is that it's one-sided. I was placed so high on her pedestal that my head was up in the clouds, feeling that I was the king of my castle. Therefore, I was incapable of providing her with the love that she and every woman needs to receive from the man who has pledged to love and cherish her for life.

Even the best woman on the planet will tire of giving and never receiving much in return. And it all came crashing down around me because she, ultimately, became angry and bitter at me for failing to meet her needs in return. Her anger towards me was fueled by the fact that she felt she created a monster, and then she became disgusted with the monster of her own creation. After a while, the only thing she wanted to do was to get away from Frankenstein's monster—pun intended.

So, when she exploded in anger, I was thoroughly confused. When she entered into a relationship with a guy at her job and started spending nights and entire weekends with him because she no longer cared about my feelings, I was nonplussed at her newfound careless and insensitive attitude. In fact, the only person Bev cared about during that stretch was Bev. I was getting a dose of my own medicine, and I deserved it, but I hated it nonetheless.

She was convinced that I was so self-centered that I was incapable of changing. She determined that a lifetime with me would be a lifetime of misery. Even though I cried, begged, and pleaded for a second chance, it was all for naught because she had drawn a line in the sand and had thrown in the towel on the marriage. She felt used, abused, and taken for granted. She felt that she had invested in me and had received no return on her investment. She was angry for wasting that kind of time and energy on someone whom she felt did not deserve it.

Bev's problem was not confined to the fact that I didn't get it, which was true, but it was equally true that she didn't "get it" either. She didn't know that she needed to teach me how to love her because I wasn't getting it on my own. She thought that by spoiling me and showering me with love and affection, I would "get it" by osmosis.

Ladies, listen to me: that rarely happens. Read my lips: a selfish, self-centered, self-aggrandizing man, which is what I was at the time, rarely ever gets it on his own—without a catalyst! Men typically do not change without one.

You are important. Your needs are important. It's not selfish to want your man to love you. It's permissible for you to tell him that you're not happy. Disturb his comfort zone. By all means, you must reveal how unhappy you are—you must. Stop being afraid to upset him. If calling him on the carpet is going to save the marriage, then for God's sake, call him on the carpet, read him the riot act, whatever. Just do it.

However, you must do it in such a way that you don't turn him off. It requires a certain skillset. So, if you must enroll in my course to learn the "art of teaching your man to love you the way you want to be loved," then so be it. Your happiness and the wellbeing of your marriage and family is worth the sacrifice.

How long can your marriage last if he's living in marital bliss because you've made him think that all is well with the marriage when you actually are quite miserable and are withholding your true feelings because you are afraid that he might get upset if you divulge that information? If telling him that he must improve as a husband is the catalyst that he needs to change, then so be it.

Please, please, learn from the mistakes that both Beverly and I made. I am desperately trying to prevent you from going down the same road that we traveled. I want to spare your family the heartache that my family experienced. The saddest part about it is this: I'm convinced that it could have and would have been avoided if only Bev and I had made better, more informed choices and decisions. I'm revealing the pitfalls that can sabotage your marriage. By all means, avoid them like the plague.

Create his Catalyst

Let me put it to you this way to make it more palatable for your emotional digestion: if a man's family has spoiled him rotten from birth and caused him to think that his stuff does not stink, and then you come along and elevate him even higher on that palatial pedestal, what makes you think he's just going to suddenly "get it?"

No, that's not happening. You need to help him. He needs a catalyst. He will forever remain in "king of the castle" mode focused on his own needs unless you threaten his comfort zone. That, my friend, is a catalyst. Most selfish men will never love you the way you deserve without one.

A catalyst is a life-altering situation that threatens our comfort zone and effectively convinces us that we need to change. It's a situation that causes a man to realize that he is about to lose you forever because of his unwillingness to love you on your terms! A catalyst is when you either leave him or threaten to leave. A catalyst is when you inform him that you no longer love him—or worse yet—that you are falling or have fallen in love with someone else. Unfortunately, it is not until he is threatened with losing you that he truly realizes that he must change his modus operandi.

The typical man, who is self-absorbed in his own world, does not wake up one day and realize on his own that he must undergo a radical change in the way he loves and treats his wife or girlfriend. However, if he loves you, if he cares about you, the one thing that will turn his life upside down and have him on his knees, begging you for a second chance to demonstrate to you that he can love you the way you want to be loved, is a catalyst!

I've assisted so many women with crafting their particular catalysts that I've lost count. When he truly loves you, the turn-around is instantaneous and almost MIRACULOUS! I've seen the most insensitive, the most selfish, the most self-absorbed, callous men in a matter of days, minutes, or sometimes even seconds, begin crying, groveling, and begging on their knees desperately asking for a second chance to get it right and to save the relationship.

I will add that when he loves and cares for you, although you may not feel loved, the change is virtually instantaneous. I have firsthand experience.

My catalyst was when Bev came home and declared the marriage was over, started sleeping with another man, and spent entire weekends with him. Talking about a catalyst, it was all the impetus I needed. It instantaneously pimp-slapped me in the face. Immediately, my whole world was disturbed; my comfort zone was gone. Realizing that I was about to lose that which was the most important thing in the world to me, and that I was the cause, was all the catalyst I needed. I was forced to change, or I would lose the one person who meant more to me than any human being on the planet.

I was ready to change. In fact, I did change. Realizing that I was in a battle, I began doing all the right things: I sent flowers and cards to her job. I took her to dinner in an effort to demonstrate that I was capable of loving her on her terms. I realized that I could not remain the selfish man that I had been for the previous 12 years of our marriage. I finally got it. But, for me, it was too little, too late.

Teaching your man how to love you is unavoidable because the love of selfish men is not other-centered—which is where it must be if you are to experience happiness in the relationship. It's self-centered.

Most men are not going to just get it on their own. Most men are not going to have this awesome epiphany, this life-changing revelation that changes them overnight. We both know that's a fairytale, and fairytales aren't true. You need to help him be what you need him to be for you. Most importantly, you need to help him be what God wants him to be—starting with your marriage or relationship.

The Importance of Your Role

Now, I know what some of you are thinking. I can almost hear your thoughts: why is that my job? Why do I have to treat him like he's my son instead of him acting like he's my man? Why can't he love me the way I love him?

Can I answer that for you once and for all? Here it is: it's instinctive for you.

It's second nature for you to love, cherish, pamper, and nurture. God created women with incredible virtues and characteristics. They are preprogrammed into your psyches at birth. Women don't have to work at love—you just love! Women typically never have to put forth much effort when it comes to giving, sharing, and pampering; it's your nature. Those traits are visible in females even at an early age.

Case in point, several years ago my son, Damon, came to town and brought three of his four children: Xavier, 16; Dasia, 14; and the baby, little Damon, who was a year and a half at the time. For the couple of days that they were with us, one of the two teenagers met every need of their baby brother. One of them fed him, bathed him, and changed his Pampers. Now, they both loved him, played with him, and interacted with him. But there was just one of my two teenage grandchildren that was nurturing and functioning as the primary caregiver from the time they came to the time they left. Which one do you think it was: Xavier, my grandson, or Dasia, my granddaughter? The answer should be obvious without me providing it.

I think it's safe to say that God created women with specific characteristics to prepare you for motherhood. Because you give birth to children, God has endowed you with all of the requisite characteristics that motherhood requires. Consequently, you are loving, kind, patient, longsuffering, nurturing, understanding, comforting, and the list goes on. On top of that, for many of you, your formative years serve as a veritable training ground where you receive plenty of practice "mothering and nurturing" your siblings and caring for the family at large in several capacities, be it cooking, washing, cleaning, babysitting, etc.

But, unfortunately for guys, most of us are raised differently than the typical female. Most of us have no training ground in our formative years that requires us to care for anyone other than ourselves. Rather than requiring us to be other-centered and selfless, many of us are taught early that it's a man's world.

In many homes, the workload is placed mainly on you at the exclusion of your brothers, especially if you are the oldest sibling. To add injury to insult, it's quite often that you do things for your brothers that they should do for themselves.

And if you refuse to take advantage of the opportunity to train your man how to love you the way you want to be loved, then I must share with you the consequences of your behavior. Permit me to break it to you gently. Some teaching is going on, but unfortunately, you are not the teacher—you are the student! If you are not teaching him to love you the way you want to be loved, then rest assured that you are being taught to accept him the way that he is, in all of his selfishness. He's teaching you how to focus the attention on him. He's teaching you how to meet his every need. I know because that's how I functioned for a very long time.

Ladies, you, typically, approach marriage and relationships much more prepared to hold up your end of the bargain, whereas the typical male has the disadvantage of thinking that people should do for him and give to him. When the two of you meet and form a relationship, the outcome is inevitable:

you, typically, will be the giver, while he will be the receiver. I can almost guarantee it.

Because no one has taught him otherwise, he doesn't know any other way of thinking and acting. Therefore, if you don't help him, he is incapable of "getting it" on his own. Except for a very rare, once-in-a-very-blue-moon occasion, he remains incarcerated in his self-centered prison. And if he is ever to be freed from that prison, you must become his liberator and set him free from such "stinkin' thinkin'."

Not only are some of you guilty of placing your man's needs before yours without ever being the recipient of his love, but far too many of you are guilty of placing your children's needs before your own as well. I've had conversations with women who have confessed that they've neglected their own needs so their children could have the latest and best of everything. Some of you wear worn-out bras, run-down shoes, holey stockings—and I don't mean righteous ones either. And if you sacrifice and buy something for yourself, some of you will feel so guilty you'll actually take it back to the store! Are you serious?

In essence, you have become the slave to everyone in the house. You look out for everyone else's needs, while no one else responds in kind. When your man consistently fails to meet your needs, both your happiness and your health can be compromised. Far too many of you think that everyone in the house is more important than you. Stop it. That mindset can and will crack open a door to a life-threatening illness and disease, which can kill you! You deserve to love and pamper yourself sometimes. You're worth it.

Lessons Learned

Now, back to my story. Beverly left me for the other guy. I hung in for a long time. I cried and pleaded with her to come home because I was a changed man. When I heard she was pregnant, I called her and appealed to her that she could come home—even pregnant with another man's child, I informed her that I would love her and the child and would raise and love him or her as my own. I meant every word of it. Unfortunately, I never was given that chance.

When reality set in and I realized that Bev was never coming back, I sought and secured a divorce so I could go on with my life. And because I definitely wanted to succeed at something that was so important, I wanted to avoid the same mistakes I had made in my first marriage. I wanted to be the best man and husband that I could be.

During that period of soul-searching, I realized that my deep-seated flaws single-handedly ruined a good marriage. I pledged that I would never let that happen again. I meant it. I wanted to be the most loving, caring man on the planet. I was ready for marriage—or so I thought.

Six years had passed when I met Angela. She walked into the room with her awesome head of red hair. I was the only male presenter at a single's retreat in November 1991. I said to myself, "Who is that?" She blew me away. She was one of the nicest, kindest, sweetest women I had ever met in my life. I chased her the entire weekend. Notwithstanding that she was seeing someone, we were an item within seven days. There was no way I was going to let her get away. I had to have her as my life's mate.

After deciding that I never wanted to fail at a relationship again, you would think that coming into this marriage, I would finally "get it," right? Wrong, I didn't.

The first seven years of our marriage were absolutely terrible. I concluded that I had made a mistake and that I was not going to remain in the midst of that mistake forever.

Angela was the problem—or so I thought. I blamed her for everything. It was all her fault. If only she had loved me the way I wanted to be loved. If she met all my needs the way I was accustomed to having them met, then maybe there was an outside chance that we really could make it. But for that to happen, she had to make some significant changes. And if she wouldn't or couldn't make me happy, I was ready and willing to walk. After all, there were plenty more fish in the sea.

My selfish attitude stems from the fact that I grew up thinking that life was all about me. Not having been cured from that illness, I brought all of that baggage into my marriages. Consequently, I doomed the first and almost succeeded in sabotaging the second.

I can declare with all honesty that my hat is off to Angela because if I were her, I would not have stayed married to me—not after all I put her through. No woman should have to put up with such stupidity and immaturity. I was a bona fide, card-carrying idiot. I am forever in her debt. Because she was such an awesome woman, she saved me from myself and another failed marriage. She was so much better than me that it's ridiculous. I'm truly fortunate to have had her. My love for her knows no bounds. I don't know where I'd be without her. She helped transform me into the man that I am. To God be the glory.

Even though I lost her to COVID in 2021, I am the beneficiary of having been the man on her arm for 30 years. She truly changed my life.

But it certainly wasn't always this way. Sometime during that seventh year, we both reached the end of the line. The marriage was on its last legs because even Saint Ann, as I referred to her, was getting tired of my act. God convinced me that I had not held up my end of the bargain, that Angela was not the problem—I was. I was floored at that revelation.

God was not done with me. In fact, He was just getting started. Class had started, and I was enrolled in a new course designed to teach me how to love and treat my wife the way she wanted to be loved.

How did we make it to our 29th year of marriage? It's because of a couple of things that happened as a result of that long road trip to Maine. Remember when my wife challenged my manhood and called me to be the priest of our home? The first game changer was that I began to pray and asked God to teach me how to love my wife. I shouldn't have been surprised that the Lord had taken me on this incredible learning experience because Christ Himself says, "Ask and it shall be given."

The keyword here is TEACH! The Lord began to provide me with a level of instruction that I needed to change my flawed, self-centered outlook about marriage and relationships. The Almighty began to educate me about how men were to treat their wives.

One of the first places the Master directed me to was the book of Ephesians 5. When I read verse 25, I was convicted immediately. It was instantaneous.

In the passage, God says to all men and husbands, "Husbands, love your wives, even as Christ also loved the church, and gave himself for it." What a revelation that was. My eyes were beginning to open, and I could see that I was completely out of order. I was supposed to love her, but instead, I was requiring her to love me. No wonder we were having issues.

I looked at the rest of that verse. I noticed something that still speaks to me even to this very day. The Apostle Paul counsels men that we must treat our wives the way Christ treated His wife, and in case you're confused, His wife is the Christian Church. That's the standard for us. This instruction is especially important for any man that has not grown up with a father and has no picture of what it looks like to be a good husband and father in his home.

In essence, Ephesians 5 is functioning like a pre-marriage manual. It's like getting marriage counseling from the best marriage counselor in existence. The Word is saying to men, if you don't know how to treat a woman, then treat your woman the way Christ treated His, and your wife will be a happy camper. Why? Because Christ is the quintessential husband. So, if we simply follow His lead and treat our wives like He treated His wife, their happiness will know no bounds.

Not having exhausted the truths in that same text, the Apostle says that we should love our wives as Christ loved the Church and gave himself for it. The more I read it, the more the words began to sink in. Ladies, if you want your man to learn how to treat you, he must live out of this chapter. He must master the principles, the actions, and behaviors of the Savior. Even if he grew up without a mentor to teach him the virtues of manhood, God's word is more than adequate to fill that void.

If he begins to do a careful study of this pericope, he will discover that Christ was the lover, not the loved. Moreover, the Master was the GIVER, not the one given to. If he's paying attention, your man will realize that Christ was the one doing the sacrificing, not the one for whom the sacrifice was made. Clearly, Christ's wife, the Church, did not give nor sacrifice for Him. He did the loving, the giving, and the sacrificing. Consequently, if you are doing the loving, the giving, the pleasing, and the sacrificing, you will have issues in your relationship. It's inevitable.

I took another huge leap forward in understanding my role in marriage when God introduced me to the awesome book, *Woman's True Desire*, which I mentioned in an earlier chapter. Danièle Starenkyj writes in such a compelling way that she changed my life forever. This book crystalized issues more than any other author I'd ever read on the subject.

Completely in harmony with God's word, particularly Ephesians 5, Starenkyj taught me that a "Man's role is to LOVE, to GIVE love. It is written in his genes."[8] The book reinforces the fact that the man is the lover, the giver, and the one who does the sacrificing. This approach to marriage and relationships was exactly what I needed when I needed it. And as usual, God was right on time. However, He was not through with the process of teaching me how to love my wife.

---

8 Danièle Starenkyj, Women's True Desire, p. 42

Because *Woman's True Desire* is a book written by a woman for women, she addresses a woman's role as well. The author adds that "A woman's role is to BE loved, to RECEIVE love, it is written in her genes."[9] For the first time in my life, I felt like I was "getting it." Wow, what a revelation that was for me.

If your man follows this blueprint, your happiness goes through the roof, and you will respond to him in kind. I guarantee it.

But check this out: the more I prayed to the Lord to teach me how to love my wife, the more information He placed in my path. Knowledge began to drop in my lap, and God still wasn't through teaching me yet. Knowing my passion to teach and to disseminate information once it touches my life, the Master provided me with the information I would need to positively influence my marriage as well as enable me to share this with others so they, too, could experience what I was now enjoying.

The Master wanted me to go to yet another level in my educational process. Therefore, He permitted me to attend The Voice In The Wilderness Mission in Savoy, Massachusetts right around that time. The Mission, as mentioned previously, was the most incredible health sanitarium on earth, in my opinion. Each morning, Vernon and Sheree Dawson, the practitioners, conducted devotion to teach the clients how to live a healthy lifestyle. It was during those morning devotions that I was introduced to the book *Woman's True Desire*. It was here that I discovered the third reason why men traditionally "don't get it."

---

9 Danièle Starenkyj, *Women's True Desire,* p. 41

There was a statement in *Woman's True Desire* that blew me away. Did you notice in each of the statements above concerning how both men and women are to treat each other, the author adds the words "it is written in his genes" and "it is written in her genes?"

Starenkyj is addressing the fact that on a biological, reproductive level, God has preprogrammed both men and women to function in a certain way when we are in relationship with one another. When you follow God's marital and relational blueprint, and teach your man to love you on your terms, not his, your relationship will be blessed.

Action Plan
FOR CHAPTER 4

Please reflect on the lessons I've learned and shared here with you. Also, consider these action steps as you understand the importance of your role to become a catalyst for the man in your life:

1. Teach him to love you the way you want to be loved—no ifs, ands, or buts! You must teach him to love you ON YOUR TERMS—NOT HIS! It is the starting point for your happiness. You must learn how to do this. Many of you, if not most of you, will not be happy until you learn how to accomplish this.

2. Insist on being happy. You must change as well as your man. But, in order for that to happen, things must change. He must change, and you, my dear, must see to it! You must teach him that you are worthy of his time and attention. First and foremost, you must explain to him that you are not happy and why. Secondly, you must share what you need from him that would make you happy (reference the statement you wrote for chapter two's action plan for the exercise titled "My Husband/Boyfriend Will"). Let him know that you are more than confident he is capable of accomplishing

those things because he did them to win your heart originally. If he thinks you're being selfish or refuses to cooperate, then you must go to plan B.

3. Create a catalyst and implement it. I am certain that, in most cases, your situation will not change without one. The more self-absorbed he is, the more you must disturb his comfort zone. Most self-centered men need a catalyzing event that convinces them that if they don't change right now, they will lose the best thing that has ever happened to them—namely, YOU! You must explain that you will no longer tolerate being loved on his terms and not yours. You must inform him that not being loved the way you want to be loved is not an option. Your words, tone of voice, and body language must send the message that things must change—now! He must arrive at the conclusion that the relationship will not continue as usual. He must know that he needs to be more attentive in meeting your needs, and if not, he will notice a change in you.

4. Negotiate from a position of strength. I want you to know that if you are very unhappy or, worse yet, miserable, your typical means and methods of getting him to love you on your terms are doomed to fail. Why? Because they cause you to negotiate from a position of weakness. If you are cursing, fussing, and fighting because you are not being loved the way you desire, I must inform you that none of these things work

long-term. They may get him to change temporarily, but they rarely, if ever, bring about permanent change.

Stop negotiating from weakness; negotiate from strength. Demonstrate the behavior you want him to emulate and then teach him how to reciprocate. For example, when you're out shopping, buy him something. When you present it, it must become a teaching moment.

Say to him, "I saw this and thought you needed it or would appreciate this. Now, do you see how I thought of you? Well, guess what? I'm the same way. I love receiving gifts from you, especially when it's not my birthday or a special day. It lets me know that you are thinking of me." You must also explain how it makes you feel to receive gifts "just because."

Most importantly, you must explain the positive outcome. Please explain that when he performs random acts of kindness, you are so drawn to him that it causes you to want to reciprocate and demonstrate your love to him in the best way you know how—physically! You must show him that he gets what he needs in abundance only after you get what you need. This is the selling point that you must drive home.

5. Love yourself first. It's an absolute necessity. After all, if you don't love you, why should anyone else? Stop putting yourself on the back burner. Take care of yourself.

Protect yourself. Fight for yourself and your happiness. Stop suffering in silence hoping that your man one day has this incredible epiphany and realizes that he is not loving you the way you want to be loved. You deserve to be happy too. You are as entitled to be happy as every other member of your family. Stop placing everyone before you.

If and when he balks at the changes that you need him to make to ensure your happiness, you must stand your ground. Don't be intimidated unless you are forced to because he has threatened you with bodily harm or worse. Be smart here. If you sense danger or the threat of violence, don't be a martyr. Live to see another day. Don't try to prove your toughness—get to safety first. Once you've separated yourself from him, be tough over the phone! Don't be a hero unnecessarily.

But please know that most men will not change voluntarily without a catalyzing event of some kind. I will not spell out what those are. I always leave that to my clients to determine because every case is different.

However, if you do nothing, most likely, he will do nothing. Most men balk at changing until they are threatened with losing that which is nearest and dearest to them. Most men resist change until their comfort zones are disturbed because you withhold something he desires or you cease doing some of the things that you've always done. When a man no longer has the same privileges that he loves and does not want to be without, trust me. You will get his attention.

I realize that many of you will need help with this. Therefore, feel free to access my website, www.theartof-womanhood.org, and let's get you the help you need.

CHAPTER 5

CROSSING BARRIERS

The Eve Syndrome

I contend that many women have a fatal flaw that they are probably unaware of. To explain it, I must take you back to the Garden of Eden. As we take a close look at this story, I think we'll discover that when compared with women of yesteryear, today's women really aren't that different.

As we carefully examine the creation story, we find that God creates a man and calls him Adam and then creates a woman whom Adam names Eve. Both Adam and Eve were clearly instructed regarding the one tree which was off-limits. Under no circumstances were they to even touch it, let alone consume it. Eve, the initial culprit and this world's first violator, explains to the serpent as much in Genesis 3:2-3, "We may eat of the fruit of the trees of the garden: But of the fruit of the tree which is in the midst of the garden, God hath said, Ye shall not eat of it, neither shall ye touch it, lest ye die."

It is significant that Satan targeted Eve as opposed to Adam in his fiendish scheme to entice the holy pair to distrust God and subsequently disobey Him, thus opening the door to sin and woe. My favorite author, Ellen G. White, says this about the Garden experience, "Satan was not to follow them with continual temptations; he could have access to them only at the forbidden tree."[10]

To maximize their safety, God placed the couple in a safe zone. They were, if you will, placed in a bubble. They were insulated from the archenemy of their souls. Other than in the immediate vicinity of the Tree of knowledge of Good and Evil, the Garden of Eden was literally a barrier that Satan was powerless to cross. He couldn't get to them. The one and only way that he could have access to them is if one or both came to him. And tragically one of them did. Guess who?

Satan did his homework. While unable to follow them into the Garden itself, he did the next best thing. He studied them. He watched their tendencies, their likes and dislikes. He took note of their personalities and their temperaments.

Having done that, Satan determined that the woman would be an easier target, an easier prey than her husband. Therefore, Satan set his trap, which was targeted especially for the woman, and waited. White, referring to the forbidden tree, declares, "Should they attempt to investigate its nature, they would be exposed to his wiles. They were admonished to give careful heed to the warning which God had sent them and to be content with the instruction which He had seen fit to impart."[11]

---

10 Ellen G. White, *Patriarchs and Prophets,* Review and Herald Publishers: Hagerstown, MD, p. 53

11 Ellen G. White, *Patriarchs and Prophets,* p. 53

Lo and behold, Eve ventures unsuspectingly into the danger zone—alone and unprotected.

Satan, assuming the form of a serpent, speaks to her. Her curiosity is piqued. The serpent, as the instrument of temptation, was no accident. It was carefully chosen for the occasion for it was exquisitely ornamented and decorated—obviously quite pleasing to her eye.

When a woman sets her eyes on the prize, she sees little else. Ladies, be careful, be very careful of what I refer to as the "Eve Syndrome," which is the desire to acquire something at all costs.

Eve knew the fruit was forbidden, but that didn't stop her. Many have asked the age-old question, "Why was she so determined to consume that which God specifically warned her not to?"

Here's why: the Bible declares that sin comes in three flavors. 1 John 2:6 describes it this way, "For all that is in the world, the lust of the flesh, the lust of the eyes, and the pride of life."

Eve violated because she saw what she wanted and was determined to have it. There was no stopping her. God had already warned her that it was not in her best interest to partake of the forbidden fruit, but somehow that meant nothing to her.

There was a clearly defined boundary placed before her. It was the Tree of Knowledge of Good and Evil. It was off-limits. But, Satan successfully dangled a carrot before her that was so desirous that she was willing to turn her back on God to get it. The fruit became all-consuming to her. She was willing to do anything to get it—and she did—at the cost of her life and the lives of her husband and offspring.

By accepting Satan's lie that God was withholding something from her, Eve concluded that God had, in effect, lied to her and her husband. Backing herself into Satan's corner of deception, Eve reasoned that if God was willing to lie and withhold something from them, it had to be worth having. It had to be worth the risk of disobeying his unambiguous instructions and warnings of death.

Eve rationalized that being a sinless human being was not good enough. Because there was more to be had, she wanted more. Because of her newfound friend, she ignored God's clearly defined instructions and arrived at the erroneous conclusion that rather than merely being a sinless human being, she could be a goddess. She bought Satan's lie that she could become equal to God. She willfully, recklessly ran through the boundary by partaking of forbidden fruit.

And the rest is history.

Her actions were totally inexcusable. God had provided the pair with everything they could ever want in life. But for Eve, enough was not enough. Convinced that there was more to life, she was not about to settle for less. Her fatal flaw reared its ugly head when she crossed a boundary that she knew was off-limits.

There it is—a woman's fatal flaw. It's a woman's propensity to pursue that which is not always in her best interest. It's her insatiable desire to have that "one thing" that becomes all-encompassing. It's that voice that whispers in her ear, "You must have this no matter the sacrifice, no matter the cost."

There was no reason why Eve should have been tempted to want more than God had provided for her and her husband.

She was perfect. Her husband was perfect. Their home and surroundings were perfect. She wanted for nothing.

But somehow, mysteriously, she was not satisfied with her place in life. Somehow, she wanted more and was willing to risk all to get it.

She was willing to cross a forbidden threshold, which in this case was the safety and security of the Garden, fall hard for Satan's line, and in the process instantly distrust the God she had heretofore loved with all her heart and soul. After this chance meeting, she was instantly convinced that God, in His selfishness, had withheld something from her that she couldn't live without. So, like a bull in a china shop, she recklessly charged through a barrier that was erected and designed to protect her and her husband. How and why was she willing to sacrifice everything for someone she just met? Why was she willing to climb any mountain, jump any hurdle, run through any barrier for a complete stranger—and a snake at that? Better yet, why was she so easily convinced that God had lied to her by withholding a better state of godliness, when prior to this encounter with the enemy of her soul, she had never felt deprived of anything?

In the book *Patriarchs and Prophets*, a must-read if ever there was one, White adds this valuable insight: "Eve had been perfectly happy by her husband's side in her Eden home; but, **like restless modern Eves**, she was flattered with the hope of entering a higher sphere than that which God had assigned her. In attempting to rise above her original position, **she fell far below it**."[12]

---

12 Ellen G. White, *Patriarchs and Prophets*, p. 59

Eve reached for the heavens and missed. In an attempt to elevate herself above her current place in life, she experienced a dramatic and traumatic fall as a consequence. God shows clearly in Genesis 3:16 that there are consequences for violating God's will. Those consequences take you down; they never elevate you to a higher plane in life—never. Genesis 3:16 reads, "Unto the woman he said, I will greatly multiply thy sorrow and thy conception; in sorrow thou shalt bring forth children; and thy desire shall be to thy husband, and he shall rule over thee."

God made a safe place for her as wife, mother, and queen of her home. But that which God established for her was not satisfactory; she wanted more. Sadly, even tragically, she was willing to risk her life for it. And as a consequence, she eventually lost everything—including her life—for something that was never in her best interest.

Consider this poignant comment: "The woman had broken her divinely appointed relationship with the man. Instead of being a help 'meet' for him, she had become his seducer. Therefore her status of equality with man was forfeited; he was to 'rule over' her as lord and master."[13]

Ladies, you cannot miss the point here. God ordained that Eve would function as the "helpmeet" to her husband; that was her divinely ordained role. She was to be Adam's designated cheerleader, motivator, and source of inspiration. She had been specifically placed in his life so that she would

---

13 Nichol, F. D. (Ed.). *The Seventh-day Adventist Bible Commentary* (Vol. 1, p. 234). Review and Herald Publishing Association.

use her influence to take him up to higher heights for God as well as for his family. Instead, she switched roles with him.

Role Reversal

Instead of being the helpmeet, she assumed his role and became the seducer. Having taken on his role, she was now incapable of performing her own. Having taken leave of her role as helpmeet, she was now incapable of helping him be the best leader he could be. So, if she had now crossed over into the forbidden zone by failing to carry out the duty and responsibility that was clearly hers to perform, who was there to push Adam to be the best that he could be? Who inspired him to be faithful to God even in the face of temptation? Who became his Rock of Gibraltar when he buckled in the face of adversity?

Having abandoned her role as counselor, who was to stand by Adam's side as the voice of reason when the enemy came rushing in like a flood? Who would be there for the Adams of the world? Who would appeal to him that he should be faithful to God even amidst the most dire circumstances?

Without his helpmeet to help direct him in the paths of righteousness, Adam was more vulnerable than he had ever been. Because Eve had abandoned her calling in life, Adam had no light to illuminate his path, no GPS to guide his direction, no tour guide to keep him on the straight and narrow. His support system was gone. For him, it was like a pilot flying an aircraft when the entire instrument panel goes out. He was flying blindly, and to add injury to insult, the fuel tank was on empty. Consequently, there was only one direction in which the aircraft, the passengers, and the crew could go, and that was downwards.

By stepping out of her support role and assuming Adam's headship role, Eve did irreparable harm to her man. Yet she thought she was helping him. Nothing could have been further from the truth. And ladies, you aren't helping your man either when you assume his role as the head of the home, by making the decisions for the family that he should be making. Plus, when the children regard you as the leader of your home and they completely dismiss him, you have problems.

By permitting your man to abdicate his responsibilities in the family, your actions are actually stunting his growth and impeding his development as the head of the home. The worst part about it is that the longer you remain in that role, the longer he will allow you. Thus, the problem is compounded over time.

What amazes me is that it is becoming increasingly popular for women to change roles with their men, like Eve changed roles with Adam, and yet hope to have a different experience. It reminds me of what is said about the definition of insanity: *doing the same thing over and over again and expecting to get a different result.* Do you get the point?

Once Eve carelessly ran out of her lane, partook of the forbidden fruit, and coaxed her husband to join her in rebellion, God, in His infinite wisdom, concluded that for the protection and safety of women, a new arrangement was necessary in marriage, and it was instituted immediately after Eve and Adam sinned.

As a result and direct consequence of Eve's sin, God declared, in Genesis 3:16, that the woman was now subject to her husband. This new arrangement was designed to be a blessing to women—not a curse. Adam loved his wife more than he loved God, as demonstrated by his choice to join her in disobedience and death and place his loyalty to his wife before his loyalty to his creator. So, God, for the sake of Eve and all women thereafter, placed them in subjection to their husbands. There should never have been a question as to whether they would be loved, respected, and protected.

From that day forward, if all men loved their wives, even today, like Adam loved Eve, every woman on the planet would be absolutely ecstatic. Do not get it twisted, however, for I am not suggesting that men place their wives and women above God. That is blasphemy. I'm merely acknowledging Adam's immense love for his wife, which was undeniable.

Genesis 3:16 and the commentaries above allude to the consequence of Eve's sinful behavior: "And he shall rule over thee."

"Recognizing that women had the proclivity to run through barriers, God, in His omniscience, altered the status of women in their marital relationships. Prior to sin, both Adam and Eve were created equally. They were equal in status but different in role and function."[14]

But after Eve's willful disobedience, Adam is designated the leader, while Eve is designed as the follower—for the purpose of safeguarding and protecting her. As the leader, the man has clearly defined roles to fulfill, roles that are exclusively his. It

---

14 Samuele Bacchiochi, *Women In The Church,* Berrien Springs, MI, 1989, p. 31

has nothing to do with whether she's capable or not: they are the duties that God has assigned to the man to fulfill for his wife and children. Eve, nor any other woman for that matter, has not been called to fulfill the roles that God has given to the husband. If and when that happens, women suffer consequences, as did Adam and Eve with disastrous results.

Ellen G. White provides this warning to all "modern day Eves" who follow in Eve's footsteps of disobedience: "A similar result will be reached by all who are unwilling to take up cheerfully their life duties in accordance with God's plan. In their efforts to reach positions for which He has not fitted them, many are leaving vacant the place where they might be a blessing. In their desire for a higher sphere, many have sacrificed true womanly dignity and nobility of character, and have left undone the very work that Heaven appointed them."[15]

Ladies, you must understand your tendency to win at all costs. You must understand the fact that many women have the tendency to run through stoplights and stop signs. Please know that many of you have the propensity to be "in it to win it." Just know that the average woman will not stop until she gets what she wants. She'll keep going until she gets it—no matter how much pain she has to endure first.

You must understand your penchant to latch onto things and not let go. This, more than anything else that I can think of, makes you vulnerable and increases the possibility that you

---

15 Ellen G. White, *Patriarchs and Prophets*, Review and Herald Publishers: Hagerstown, MD, p. 59

will lock onto something like a pit bull and not let go until you are pried loose.

The roles that God has assigned to men are not interchangeable with women. Ladies, your family means everything to you—I get it. In an attempt to ensure that your family lacks nothing, you quite often think that you are coming to the rescue when your man, for whatever reason, decides that he cannot, or worse yet, will not be the leader and provider for the family that God has called him to be. If you attempt to carry out your responsibilities and his, both you and your family will suffer—no matter how noble your intentions are.

Ladies, I need you to understand something. If your man loses his job and refuses to work because he cannot find a job in his field that satisfies him, if you compensate by getting a second job and permit him to stay home while you take on that added burden of being the provider for your family, both you and your family will suffer consequences—even if you more than adequately replace his income.

There is more than just income at stake here. In that particular scenario, those who suffer the most are your children. Daily, they watch you slave to make ends meet while Dad watches TV or is on the computer all day. For both you and them, the consequences are endless. You cannot, you must not, permit your man to be less than a man, a leader, and the head of his home.

Please know that one half of the picture that sons and daughters need to ultimately be the men and women, husbands and wives they need to be, comes from their father. If Dad is permitted to be less than a man, then their picture of how a husband, father, provider, and leader should function in his family becomes distorted. Consequently, daughters often conclude that that's how men function. Therefore, that's what they permit when they become wives. Sons often conclude that a "good woman" will take care of him, which leads him to become a "chip off the old block." Sadly, it becomes a self-fulfilling nightmare in the family.

Instead of following the blueprint that God established for the family in Genesis 1 and 2, even godly women today are allowing societal trends to lead them in a different direction. It is indeed a direction that creates more problems for the family than it solves.

Current Societal Trends

You should know and understand that elevating worldly customs and traditions over the word of God is the exact opposite of what scripture counsels us to do. Romans 12:2 says, "Don't copy the behavior and customs of this world, but let God transform you into a new person by changing the way you think. Then you will learn to know God's will for you, which is good and pleasing and perfect."

What's wrong with taking our marching orders from society? Here's the problem: that which society endorses is almost always at odds with God and His word.

An even better question is who controls society? Consider the story in Matthew when Satan takes Christ to a very high mountain and propositions him.

The Bible declares, "Next, the devil took him to the peak of a very high mountain and showed him all the kingdoms of the world and their glory. 'I will give it all to you,' he said, 'if you will kneel down and worship me.'" **(Matt. 4:8-9).**

As he was in the 1st century, Satan is behind societal trends yet today. The problem is not just that they don't lead to God, but rather that they almost always lead away from him. I can't think of one societal trend that encourages women to have a closer walk with God.

What is happening is that society encourages women that they can do whatever a man can do. That problem is compounded by the fact that when men fail to be the heads of their homes and to fulfill their God-given roles—namely those of provider and burden bearer—women are switching roles with their men to fill the gap, which is to the detriment of themselves and their families.

One of the first, obvious, effects of reversing roles with your man is that your frustration level goes through the roof. Yes, you may become the man of the house, and for a minute, it may appear to be working. But you must realize one thing—you can't violate God's word without suffering consequences. If Adam and Eve's experience in the Garden of Eden taught us anything, it's that when you go contrary to God's plan for your life, you will pay dearly down the road as a result.

Women are adding to their already heavy loads the responsibilities of headship and all that comes with that.

Scripture is clear, "For a husband is the head of his wife as Christ is the head of the church" (Ephesians 5:23).

Headship in a family is the man's role. Not only does the Word declare, but the overwhelming majority of women, with the exception of some feminists, would agree that they do not want to "wear the pants in the family."

After coaching scores of women and after 40 years of pastoring, I've never had a woman declare that she wanted to be the head of the home and make all the decisions in addition to being the breadwinner, provider, and protector—never!

God, in His infinite wisdom, determined that the blueprint for relational and marital happiness is contingent upon the man being the head and leader of his family—not his wife.

God's blueprint for the family is designed to ensure the happiness of every member of the family. To enjoy that happiness to the fullest, you must remain in your lane, and your man must remain in his.

When I began the process of working with my daughter, we discussed how she arrived at the deplorable state that she found herself in when I called her that day. After listening intently, I discovered that she had one major flaw. She pampered and spoiled the guy she was pursuing, thinking that if she met his every need, she'd realize her number-one desire—to be swept off her feet by her knight in shining armor, walk down the aisle, stand before the preacher, her family and friends, and, most importantly, God, to exchange I do's, get married, have children, and live happily ever after. It's, essentially, every young woman's dream.

To realize that dream, she concluded that there had to be some give and take. The problem is that she was doing all the giving, and he was doing all the taking. She kept going in pursuit of her elusive dream. She saw stop signs, but she ran through them.

How? Why? Simple. My research and conversations with women, especially young women between the ages of 18–35, informed me that many women quite often continue their pursuit of their goal, even if it causes more pain than pleasure.

In her quest to experience her ultimate dream, my daughter was willing to give supremely—even if it hurt. But the problem is that the more she gave, the more he took. Yet nothing about their situation was changing.

The brother had all the meals, companionship, dedication, and commitment that she could provide him, and yet from month to month, she was no closer to her dream than when she started. Did she back off? No! She pushed ahead, thinking that because it wasn't working, the problem must have been her! Somehow, she concluded that there was something she wasn't doing right. She wrongfully concluded that she had to give more; she had to do more.

Therefore, there was more pampering, more attentiveness, more everything, all with the hope that one day, he would see what a wonderful woman he had and would come to his senses and recognize how blessed he was to have such an incredible woman in his life.

He was not the man for her. He never was. He thought he was the man. He thought he was a modern-day version of Casanova. And because she was giving, he was taking.

It was precisely at that moment while, in the midst of her discovering how foolish she had been, the Holy Spirit had whispered to me, "Call your daughter." Thank God that He did. Or else, who knows how long she would have gone on attempting to win someone who was not winnable!

The enormity of the situation had just hit home for her. She felt foolish, tarnished, used, abused, and embarrassed to say the least.

Was she completely caught off guard? She shouldn't have been. There were signs and hints along the way. Yes, there were road signs to alert her that there was imminent danger just around the curve, but she ignored them. Why? Because she was convinced that she would ultimately win.

There was no doubt in her mind that her plan, although it was placing her in emotional jeopardy, was going to succeed. For that reason, she refused to abandon the chase, even with no appreciable return on her significant investment.

Toxic Emotions

On one hand, filling the gaps or meeting unmet needs is noble because it bespeaks a woman's selflessness. It clearly indicates a woman's determination to do whatever she needs to do to take care of her family. Ladies, that is quite admirable when there is no man in your life or home!

Please understand this one thing, the Eve Syndrome, which is the process of taking on manly duties, doesn't just affect you in the dating process. It rears its ugly head in marriage if the relationship goes to the altar.

The worst part about all of this is you are placing yourself in harm's way physically. I can't tell you the number of couples that I've counseled in my career as a pastor that have come to me for help when the husband abandoned his responsibilities as the head of the home and provider of the family. As we talked, it was evident that the stress that the wife was under had increased tenfold—if not more.

How did many of those wives respond? The same way the average woman responds when men are derelict in their duties: the wife assumes many of the responsibilities of providing for and taking care of the family. It is not a load that she was ever designed to carry alone.

I've seen wives angry; I've seen tears shed and fingers pointed because the husband and father is present but still refuses to provide the leadership the family needs. The mere sight of her man still sitting on the same couch watching television that evening when she returns home from work raises the average woman's blood pressure.

Let's make this personal. Ladies, when you switch roles with your man and become the sole leader and provider for your family, which means you also assume the burdens that accompany those roles, how is your health adversely affected? What's happening to you internally when you are mad, angry, or frustrated at the fact that your partner has stopped partnering?

Dr. W. Lee Cowden, in his article, "Toxic Emotions," quite astutely explains that negative emotions are in fact negative hormones that the body secretes. When these negative hormones are secreted over long periods of time, it has a deleterious effect on the body. The article shows conclusively that:

- Prolonged anger adversely affects your **liver**.

- Prolonged grief and sadness adversely affects your **heart/lungs**.

- Prolonged fear and terror adversely affects your **kidneys**.

- Prolonged bitterness or resentment adversely affects your **gallbladder**.

- Prolonged feelings of abandonment adversely affects your **small intestine**.

- Prolonged disgust adversely affects your **stomach**.

- Prolonged confusion adversely affects your **thyroid and adrenals**.

- Prolonged low self-esteem or rejection adversely affects your **spleen and pancreas**.[16]

Look at the list of emotions carefully: anger, grief, sadness, bitterness, feelings of abandonment, disgust, confusion, and irritation. Every one of these are emotions that women ultimately feel when their men refuse to be men.

Now look closely at the negative effects of these emotions: liver problems, heart disease, and gallbladder, small intestine, and stomach issues, not to mention adrenal failure. So, when women are in violation of God's word that governs their

---

16 Dr. W. Lee Cowden, "Toxic Emotions"

relationships, they set themselves up for serious, and sometimes life-threatening, diseases.

Ladies, medical science is clear and unmistakable. As I alluded to above, when you are heartbroken, you become vulnerable and susceptible to disease.

There are several contributing factors to heart disease. One is diet and lifestyle. Some would also include genetics and hereditary factors. There is a third factor that has a profound impact on women's heart health—stress! It can and will take you out.

So, why are women being affected at such an alarming rate? When women are unhappy, they store it away, and it's difficult for them to move on. With each successive disappointment, with each rejection, the wound gets deeper and deeper.

The Bible warns us about this in Proverbs 17:22 when it says, "A merry heart doeth good like a medicine, but a broken spirit drieth the bones."

It is that broken spirit syndrome that causes a woman's health to be jeopardized when she takes on the duties and responsibilities that belongs to her man exclusively.

Set Firm Boundaries

Ladies, you must have boundaries. You must know when to say to yourself, "Okay, enough is enough." You can't be so desperate that you keep giving even though you're not receiving satisfactorily in return. At some point, you may be forced to conclude, especially if you are not yet married, that this dude is not the one for you. Reality has to set in, and you must realize that if you don't love you, then why should he?

If you don't look out for your best interest, why should your man? If you're going to wine him, dine him, sex him, and work while he stays home and watches you, why shouldn't he permit you to carry that tremendous burden?

As I stated in an earlier chapter, the Gen. 2:18 principle enables a woman to help elevate her man to his rightful position in the family. This subsequently encourages him to fulfill his roles and take care of his family. The more you push him to be better, the more you encourage, inspire, and motivate him, then the more you operate from a position of strength.

But when you merely accept his failures, when you permit him to be less than a man, when you embrace his duties and responsibilities, you are truly operating from a position of weakness.

Moreover, the longer you remain in the role of head of the home, provider, protector, etc., the more comfortable he becomes with you in that role. Consequently, the more responsibilities you will have to take on.

Please understand this one thing, the Eve Syndrome, the process of taking on manly duties, doesn't just affect you in the dating process. It rears its ugly head in marriage as well. Here's how: a woman, who has had her heart broken previously by a cheating boyfriend, meets and marries the man she concludes is the man of her dreams.

Still suffering from her fatal flaw that's never been cured, she switches roles with her new husband and begins the process of pampering and spoiling him rotten—and requiring nothing or very little in return. But this time, she justifies it because it's her husband. Her love has no boundaries. She loves incessantly. She gives until it hurts.

All the while, she fails to understand what's happening around her. All too often, her husband has inextricably decided that he doesn't have to do what scripture says a man should do—what it requires of him—and that is to be the leader of and the provider for his home.

The fact of the matter is a man was destined by God to love you! Nowhere in scripture is a women ever commanded to love her husband, nowhere. Why not? Because loving a woman is the man's role, not vice versa.

If this is the case, then why is it that so many women, like my daughter, are upside down in their relationships? It's simple: no one has taught them otherwise.

I'll conclude this chapter with this story from 1 Samuel, the story of Abigail and David. Every woman, especially every wife, should master Abigail's actions and behaviors. The bottom line is when Abigail met David, he was on a mission to commit murder, and Abigail knew it. Skillfully and artfully, she changed his mindset and his direction. She erected a standard for him to adhere to. Masterfully, she appealed to him that he was destined for great things in life and that he should not come down to her husband's level. Abigail single-handedly took David to another level in one mere encounter.

Every woman has the same ability to impact the direction of the men in their lives. God has imbued you with those same gifts. Ask God to help you to identify those gifts, and then you can require your man to be better. You've got this. You can do this because Christ said you can do all things through Christ who strengthens you (Phil. 4:13).

Action Plan
FOR CHAPTER 5

After reflecting on Eve's motivations and faulty ambitions, assess your own role in your household and the barriers and boundaries in place. Are they right? Are they firm? What changes might you need to make? Consider these questions, along with the following action steps to continue your journey of empowerment:

1. Realize that many of you—this is especially true of younger women—have a proclivity to cross barriers by taking on the roles and responsibilities of your man. Resist that urge at all costs. Refuse to allow yourself to fulfill his roles in your family.

2. Require him to be the man he needs to be. If he is your man, he should function like one. Insist that he do so if he intends on being your man! Send the message loudly and clearly that his failure to produce has caused the problem. Put the issue where it belongs, squarely at his feet. If he will not work and chooses to watch TV and be online all day, then do not pay those bills. Instruct him that if he wants them, he must GET A JOB AND PAY FOR THEM! If you pay those bills, you and your family will lose.

3. Consider his consequences. If he still refuses to work, then you may need to consider moving out for a temporary period and leaving him in the house/apartment alone. In that scenario, he will be required to get a job so he can pay the mortgage/rent, keep the lights on, buy food, and the basic necessities. If you do those things for him, then he may remain stuck forever. You must require him to be the head of your home. If he refuses to accept those responsibilities, he must suffer consequences. Being placed in dire straits is a great motivator for most people. Do not treat him like a child that needs to be cared for. He is not a baby. He's a man. Require him to be one.

4. Spend time in prayer. Make no hasty decisions, especially if you're married and have children with this man. Seek out the counsel of spiritual people you trust who will be open and honest with you. I am not advocating divorce. I would never suggest that you should divorce your husband on these grounds. However, there is no sin in attempting to help your man be a man by separating from him, at least on a temporary basis, for the purpose of giving him a catalyst to be what God has destined him to be.

Some of you will need help with this process. Consult my website, www.theartofwomanhood.org, to enroll in my coaching course and permit me to show you how to help your man be the man of his home.

CHAPTER 6

FINAL REFLECTIONS

Common Mistakes

I've identified 30 mistakes that women routinely make at the outset of a new relationship. That's right—30! Now, while no woman makes all 30 of them, I've never met, worked with, or even spoken to a woman about relationship or marriage issues that has not made many, if not all of, the first six mistakes, which are the following:

1. They routinely put men in the driver's seat of the relationship before they have earned the right to be there.

2. They begin to negotiate from a position of weakness.

3. They surrender their power to their men and end up with varying degrees of powerlessness.

4. They violate God's Biblical blueprint, which is designed to ensure relational and marital happiness.

$5.$ They simultaneously violate their biological blueprint, which is also designed, by the creator, to ensure our relational and marital happiness.

$6.$ Because of the previous five mistakes, it is inevitable that these women will now operate from a position of fear!

But, of these six, the first and most egregious of them all is mistake #1. Ladies, before I elaborate, I've also discovered that once this first mistake is made, the next five drop like dominos. It's automatic.

The first mistake that practically every woman makes is putting a man in the driver's seat of the relationship before he has earned the right to be there. From the outset of a new relationship, the average woman, especially when she's in love, spoils, pampers, and places her man on a pedestal very early in the relationship. This is a huge mistake that women consistently make. Far too often these consequences last a lifetime!

When a woman permits a man to take complete control of the relationship very early on, without him being vetted by her to ascertain if he has the desire to love and cherish her the way she needs to be loved, that relationship and ultimate marriage will be all about him! As a result of this one mistake, the seeds of her marital unhappiness, misery, and possibly divorce, are sown during the dating process before they ever get to the altar, without her knowledge, as soon as they begin dating.

From working with and coaching scores of women, it's my observation that a woman at the outset of a new relationship with a man teaches her man how NOT to love her!

Additionally, because women love and shower their men with affection, everything about the relationship from the time they meet, and ultimately throughout the marriage if it goes to the altar, is all about him!

In doing so, women actually teach their men to be selfish and self-centered. Why would they do that? Because until now, no one told them not to. Women end up sabotaging their own happiness when they create an environment within the courtship, and ultimately their marriage, that focuses on his needs exclusively—not hers.

Women unknowingly create relationships and marriages where the love and affection flows in one direction from her to him. How is this happening? Why is the average woman so busy giving, loving, and pleasing her man that she fails to realize how unhappy and unfulfilled she is? Typically, although planted at the outset of a new relationship, the seeds of unhappiness may not manifest themselves until years and, in many cases, even decades later. The worst part is that, because of sheer ignorance, women end up contributing to their own unhappiness and destroying the very thing they worked extremely hard to protect—their relationship and/ or marriage. How sad.

There is a second reason why women regularly place the needs of their men before their own. Women typically give love to receive love. When the average woman experiences relational or marital unhappiness, they take the onus on themselves and conclude that it must be them. Sadly, they conclude that they must improve. They must give more, do more, please more, and sacrifice more. Because not being loved by their man is not an option, they determine that they are going the extra mile to get him to love them the way they want to be loved.

Although many should have walked away from a relationship or marriage a long time ago, for Biblical reasons, of course, many cannot or will not. They continue to love, please, and sacrifice until they can do so no longer. Some women are such diehards that, even knowing that their man is in an adulterous relationship with another woman, or worse yet, women, they still refuse to throw in the towel on the relationship. Consequently, they expose themselves to heartache and pain.

Permit me to reference my first wife, Beverly. That is exactly what happened to her. Initially, she was determined that she was going to love me into submission. She concluded, because she had to be the problem, the resolution was easy: she merely had to give more love.

However, after doing that for what must have seemed to her like an eternity, when she finally reached the conclusion that all of her efforts to love, please, and satisfy me were a waste of her time, she was devastated. She then became angry at herself for having tolerated and permitted the situation for the duration of the marriage. She concluded that because she created this problem, she was the only one that could fix it.

She felt she had created a monster who was incapable of loving her the way she needed and wanted to be loved. Now, for the sake of clarity, I was not a monster—selfish, to be sure, but I was not a monster. I loved the ground she walked on. But the problem was that Beverly was doing all the loving, giving, pleasing, and sacrificing. After a steady diet of that for 12 years, she decided that I was incorrigible and incapable of change.

She concluded—notwithstanding my tears and incessant appeals—that the only chance she'd ever have at experiencing true love again would have to be with another man. So, as painful as she knew that would be to myself, our children, our family members, church family, and inner circle of friends, she left and never returned.

Ladies, are you listening to me? Make no mistake about it. While I am not absolving myself of blame, for I acknowledge my part in ruining a good marriage, the problem began when Bev started the process of loving, pleasing, giving, and sacrificing, and thus created a one-sided marriage that left her unhappy and unfulfilled. I wish our sad story was the exception and not the rule. It is not! This same mistake is made by countless women across the globe. That women do this to themselves is standard operating procedure.

Permit me to explain how the process begins by referencing a driving metaphor.

A man and woman meet. There is a connection. She likes him; he likes her. Here is where most women make a wrong turn. Far too soon in the relationship, the woman puts the man in the driver's seat of the relationship before he has earned the right to be there.

Let me explain why that is such an egregious mistake. In a real-life driving situation, it's the driver that, **#1**, determines the **speed** and the **direction** of the relationship—not the passenger! It's the driver that determines if they will go 6 mph or 60 mph. It's also the driver that determines if they will go directly to their destination or end up hopelessly lost on a road that leads to nowhere—whether that is because he's incapable of making a decision or is simply not sure if he wants to settle down with one woman for the rest of his life.

For that woman to put that man in the position of controlling, directing, and making all the decisions for the relationship is a costly mistake for obvious reasons.

There is something else that women should consider when beginning a new relationship. Women should know that, **#2**, the driver is the one being pleased while the passenger is the **pleaser**!

For example, every time I got behind the wheel with my wife, especially if we were driving long distance, I determined what music we listened to, the temperature in the car, if we ran the AC or rolled down the windows to enjoy fresh air or blasted the heat in the winter. My wife would accommodate me in all these areas because she realized that the more comfortable she made me, the longer I'd drive. Therefore, she did her very best to please me and make me comfortable and meet my every need.

Likewise in a relationship, the passenger is the pleaser, while the driver is the one being pleased and placated. Again, on a long-distance trip, everyone in my car understood that since I was doing the heavy lifting, so to speak, I needed to be made comfortable so that I could continue to drive for hours and relieve them of that responsibility.

Consequently, ladies, you must understand that when you place the man in that seat in your life before he's earned the right to be there, you, more often than not, will end up pampering and spoiling him.

The sad part about that phenomenon is that when you begin to treat him this way, you will have to continue doing so because he will become accustomed to the treatment and will expect it.

This is exactly why many of you end up unhappy, unfulfilled, and dissatisfied with your relationship or marriage later in life.

Most importantly, I want you to understand that, **#3**, the driver dictates the terms of the relationship! He decides what's acceptable and what's not. Thus, this often leads to men becoming self-centered and self-aggrandizing.

Because of the culture that you've contributed to, your man is making all the decisions in the relationship. He determines what happens and what doesn't. He determines if marriage is an option or not.

I can't tell you the number of women who've divulged to me that after meeting Christian men, in church no less, men they liked and began to date, and a relationship began that they had high hopes for, that, after informing the men they intended to remain celibate until the wedding night, the men responded emphatically. If they wanted to be on their arm, they'd have to indulge sexually, and if not, there were plenty of other sisters in the church that would!

It should come as no shock to you that many of those same women ended up compromising—even though they knew they shouldn't. The greater problem is they were no longer making the decisions in the relationship. They mistakenly surrendered that responsibility to their men.

Ladies, please understand that men immediately go for the driver's seat in the relationship because we know from experience that the greatest benefits to us accrues from occupying that space in your lives.

Here is another consequence that you must consider: Men understand clearly and unmistakably that by occupying that space, the relationship or marriage will be about them and not you. Men know that when they occupy that place in your heart and life, the focal point of the relationship will be about what they want and need and not about you and your needs. Men are not ambiguous on this issue.

It's the male objective to occupy the driver's seat as quickly as possible. After an initial period where a few men temporarily focus on you to secure the relationship, I guarantee you that things will change soon thereafter.

Unfortunately, even the few men who begin the process of pleasing their women ultimately transition to being all about them. In short order, the relationship is about having every one of their needs met. Moreover, that will become their comfort zone. Which is why, and make no mistake about it, once men occupy the driver's seat in your life, and the satisfaction of their needs becomes paramount, it is quite difficult for many women, and impossible for others, to get their man to transition to a place where their needs take precedence. Sadly, for many men, it will never happen.

Please take note of the fact that when a woman makes mistake #1 by putting an undeserving man in the driver's seat of their relationship, mistakes 2–6 follow almost immediately.

It is a lose-lose proposition for a woman. To add injury to insult, it is the woman who gets locked in a state of unhappiness or misery merely because of a mistake she wasn't aware that she was making.

Because of this one mistake, it is the woman's happiness that suffers. It may be cute for a minute while dating to wine, dine, pamper, and spoil your man, but I guarantee that once you are doing all the loving, you will get tired of being in a relationship where the love you give flows to him in torrents, but the love he gives in return comes back to you in a trickle.

After years or even decades of never getting back what they give, many women become discouraged, disenchanted, and unhappy, which cracks the door to either an affair or ultimately divorce. The fact of the matter is it's all avoidable, especially when YOU occupy the driver's seat at the outset of the relationship.

When I coach women, this is one of the first things I teach them in my program. I teach women how to correct the first six mistakes. That is the reason why when these women master the techniques that I teach, their lives change dramatically. The power that they experience becomes liberating. So, how unfortunate is it that this knowledge is not disseminated to women the world over? How many marriages and relationships could be saved and families restored rather than being destroyed?

How prevalent is this mistake? I repeat: I've never worked with a woman who hasn't made this mistake and the ones that follow.

So, what's the explanation? I think it's a simple one. Consider this—a woman's greatest assets are simultaneously her greatest liabilities.

When a woman falls in love with a man, she must demonstrate her love in tangible ways. Therefore, she spoils him, pampers him, and puts him on a pedestal. While no one loves like a woman, her love possesses no shut-off valve—it keeps flowing even when she ought to abandon the relationship and walk away.

I spoke with one woman whose husband had left her. He had moved in with his girlfriend, who was pregnant with his baby, and he was marrying her that Sunday, but his wife wanted me to help her get him back!

When you surrender the driver's seat to undeserving men, you quite often end up vulnerable, unhappy, miserable, separated, or divorced.

So, if placing an unproven man in the driver's seat of your relationship and your heart is the problem, then what's the solution? The solution is a simple one: you MUST occupy that seat until your man has demonstrated that he has the requisite skills or desire to be everything you want and need him to be for you.

How quickly must you occupy that seat? I'll answer it this way. If you spoke with any of the women who've graduated from my "90 Days to Identify and Mesmerize the Man of Your Dreams" course, they will tell you that I teach them to occupy the seat the moment a man approaches them and expresses interest in them—that very moment!

Now to be sure, to position yourself in that position, especially never having done it before, takes a certain skillset. However, I'd have you know that there is an art to accomplish that mission, and I just happen to teach that art! So, to conclude, at the outset of a new relationship, you must occupy the driver's seat until your man has demonstrated that he is worthy of that place in your life.

Closing Remarks

In conclusion, while I believe with all my heart and soul that women are the best people on Planet Earth, that notwithstanding, most of you are contributing to your own relational or marital demise.

I've clearly seen that when you are armed with the appropriate information, you will transition from being powerless to powerful, from relational and marital unhappiness and misery to euphoria and being loved the way you want to be loved, on your terms and not his!

I started to say that the choice is yours, but that would be a poor choice of words. In reality, there shouldn't be a choice. You can no longer continue to be a woman that has unknowingly contributed to your own unhappiness merely because of relational and marital ignorance. You now have an option—a better option. It's an option that, as I've previously stated, leads to experiencing a love that you thought existed only in the movies or fairy tales.

That is what's possible for you right now. You can become the most empowered, liberated, happiest woman you've ever been in your relational or married life. But you and you alone must make that decision.

If granted the opportunity to assist you in achieving that objective, I'd be on it like a bum on a baloney sandwich—no disrespect intended. In other words, it would be an honor to work with you.

But if we should never work together, do not remain stuck. Get help. YOUR life and health depends on it.

If you need help, consult my website at www.theartof-womanhood.org

APPENDIX

In my 90-Day coaching program, **I help single Christian women over 30 experience loving relationships that exceed even their greatest expectations. Here is the syllabus for the program:**

90 Days To Identify & Mesmerize The Man of Your Dreams

Module 1

Weeks 1 & 2

Technique #1 – The Real Man Technique: I teach you to identify if a guy is Mr. Right within 30 days of meeting him.

Benefit: You will no longer date a deadbeat forever. You will be able to ascertain if he's Mr. Right or Mr. Wrong within weeks, if not days, of meeting him. Thus, no wasted time.

Weeks 3 & 4

Technique #2 – The First Encounter Technique: From the very moment you meet a guy, you will know what to say and do and, more importantly, what not to do to mesmerize, tantalize, and captivate a man.

Benefit: By using this technique, you will be completely and thoroughly in the driver's seat. In doing so, you will become the most unique woman he's *EVER MET IN HIS LIFE*. If he is Mr. Right, you will draw him like a magnet.

Week 5

Technique #3 – The Lance Armstrong/Laban Technique: This technique will demonstrate why a man MUST work for you.

Benefit: When you master this technique and require a man to work to penetrate and win your heart, not only will your relationship be blessed, but if the two of you get married, you will realize that there is a correlation between how hard he worked to get you and your happiness quotient.

Week 6

Technique #4 – The Queen of the Jungle Technique: With this technique you will learn the necessary boundaries you MUST ERECT when you meet a man who's interested in you.

Benefit: When you have clearly defined boundaries that a man should not cross, you force him to respect you and your boundaries. Immediately, it PUTS YOU IN THE DRIVER'S SEAT and separates you from other women who are "easy"— which is a turnoff to the average guy.

Module 2

Week 7

Technique #5 – Identifying the 9 Required Roles of a Godly Man: This technique does exactly what it says—it helps you to identify the 9 roles that God REQUIRES of every Godly man! This is a must for all women.

Benefit: After this session, when a man enters your life, you will forever have a standard by which to measure him. You will know which of the nine roles he is fulfilling and which ones he is not. It's one of THE MOST IMPORTANT TECHNIQUES I TEACH. PERIOD!

Week 8

Technique #6 – The Real Man Report Card Technique: This technique teaches you how to assess how your man is progressing with the 9 roles and enables you to politely address him concerning the roles and requires him to evaluate HIM-SELF to determine if he is meeting those needs!

Benefit: With laser focus, it pinpoints EXACTLY where he is as it relates to the fulfillment of the roles that God requires of him. You will now hold him to this standard. If he is deficient in any area, you will know exactly where and can address it appropriately. This technique alone WILL CHANGE YOUR LIFE!

Technique #7 – The Five Conclusions: There are five conclusions that every man makes from the first date to the altar. This technique enables you to know exactly where your man is in the relationship so that you can track his progress or the lack thereof. And one of the conclusions is a true indicator that he is into YOU! You must know which it is and must be able to recognize it.

Benefit: You will be able to recognize the language and/or the behavior associated with each conclusion. When your man has reached conclusion #3, you might need to start preparing for a wedding—I'm just saying!

Module 3

Week 9

Techniques #8 and #9 – The Nutcracker Major & Minor Techniques: What do you do when your relationship begins to fail? What do you do if your man has an affair? How do you save a dying relationship? If anything can, this technique can. It has, and it will, when mastered and done correctly.

Benefit: You will know exactly what to say and do and what not to say and do when your relationship, especially your marriage, begins to fail. You will operate from strength and not weakness. You will be the power broker in the relationship!

Week 10

Technique #10: Teaching Your Man To Love You the Way You Want To Be Loved Technique – There is an art to teaching your man to love you on your terms—you are about to learn it.

Benefit: When you teach your man to love you the way you want to be loved, if he wants to be the man on your arm, he will love you that way. When that happens, your happiness quotient goes into the stratosphere.

Technique #11 – Marriage in the Driver's Seat: If it's your desire to experience a love that's greater, deeper, and more fulfilling than anything you've ever experienced in your life, then you need to experience marriage in the driver's seat. Because, once you do, you'll never go back.

Benefit: Even though you switch roles with your man officially on wedding day, so that he's sitting in the driver's seat, because Ephesians 5:23 says, "For the husband is the head of the wife...," the benefit of having occupied that seat and correcting the mistakes you previously made is that you will have taught your man to love you the way you want to be loved. That alone will change the trajectory of your marriage and will enable you to experience a happiness, the likes of which you never thought possible. Why? It's because you will have sensitized him to regularly and consistently meeting your needs—not just his own. When implementing the technique properly, he will learn to be the lover, giver, and the pleaser that you've always desired in your man.

My experience is this. For the single woman who meets and exchanges "I do's" on wedding day, because of your new skillset, your man changes. When he changes, the relationship changes. He is much more attentive to meeting your needs than any man who came before him. Likewise, with my married clients. I regularly receive testimonials that, long after they've finished my course, their husbands routinely awaken with a list of things to fulfill each morning, and at the VERY TOP OF THAT LIST is to LOVE, CHERISH, and PLEASE YOU! That is the ultimate benefit of sitting in the driver's seat and mastering and implementing this technique at the very beginning of a new relationship.

Week 11

Technique #12 – Mastering The Abigail Technique, pt. 1: With this technique, you will learn the life-changing template to change the trajectory of your relationship. When you master this technique, you will change the man in your life.

Benefit: When your man changes, your relationship changes. When your relationship changes, your happiness quotient soars. You will become more powerful and effective than you've ever been in any relationship!

Week 12

Technique #12 continued – Mastering The Abigail Technique, pt. 2: What impact does God expect you to have on your man? You will find out with this technique, which is the queen of all techniques.

Benefit: You will discover the incredible, life-changing impact God EXPECTS you to have on your man's life. When you truly master this technique, you will become the altimeter in his life. And the best part is you help him to be better than he's ever been—WITHOUT EVER RAISING YOUR VOICE!

Bonus Session for Single Women

Bonus Technique – The Bait & Switch Technique: How do you get a man to pursue you even when there are scores of other women all vying for his attention? How do you stand out from the crowd? How do you draw him to you? There is an art to it, and I will teach the art. Ooh, the plot thickens.

Benefit: With this technique, when done properly, you go to the front of the line in 120 seconds or less!

For more information access this website:
theartofwomanhood.org

ACKNOWLEDGEMENTS

To my Lord and Savior Jesus Christ for enabling me to minister to awesome women the world over.

To my children—especially my daughters, family, and friends, who convinced me that I needed to write this book and share my knowledge with women everywhere.

To my wife, Angela, for permitting me to spend countless hours in my office working on project after project. This wouldn't be possible without your patience and understanding.

To my mother, Ora Legette, for always motivating, inspirating, and pushing me to be the best that I can be. Thank you for instilling in me that "the sky is the limit." If I accomplish anything in my lifetime, it will be because you single-handedly convinced me that there is nothing I couldn't do. Thanks, Mom, you're the best.

To Esther Pond, Sherma Green, Esther Mondesire, Pam Walker, Vera McClatchie, Sherrita Henry, Marthe Bishop-Mc-Donald, Yvonne Wickham, Alexandra Nightingale, and Stacey Grant-Montanez. These amazing women afforded me the opportunity to conduct my very first extended group session, thus officially launching my Flower Training Academy Winter

Park Chapter. As a result of the time we spent together, I concluded, relative to the future potential of this program, that I should "go big or go home." Because of your enthusiastic response to the material, I decided to go big.

To Mesago Kebaetse, my women's ministries director, whom I asked for the opportunity to address the women of our church after my daughter convinced me to share my knowledge. She graciously provided me that opportunity, and in that setting, it was truly confirmed that the Lord graced me with a knowledge about womanhood and relationships that I could not keep to myself. The rest is history. Thanks, Mesago.

My next book, *The 9 Required Roles of A Godly Man*, will help you identify the 9 roles God has designed for men and teach you how to support them in your man.

If you'd like to know what the 9 Roles are, please consult my website, www.theartofwomanhood.org.

BIBLIOGRAPHY

Bacchiochi, Samuele. *Women In The Church*. Berrien Springs, MI: 1989.

Colbert, Don. *Deadly Emotions*. Nashville, TN: Thomas Nelson Publishers.

Cowden, W. Lee. "Toxic Emotions."

Maté, Gabor. *When The Body Says No*. Hoboken, NJ: John Wiley & Sons Inc.

Nichol, F. D., ed. *The Seventh-day Adventist Bible Commentary*. Review and Herald Publishing Association, 1:234.

Starenkyj, Danièle. *Women's True Desire*. Richmond, Quebec: Ulverton House Publications.

White, Ellen G. *Adventist Home*. Hagerstown, MD: Review and Herald Publishing Association.

White, Ellen G. *Patriarchs and Prophets*. Hagerstown, MD: Review and Herald Publishers.